Guide to
Quebec Catholic Parishes
and
Published Parish
Marriage Records

by
Jeanne Sauve White

Printed for
Clearfield Company, Inc. by
Genealogical Publishing Co., Inc.
Baltimore, Maryland
1993

Reprinted for
Clearfield Company, Inc. by
Genealogical Publishing Co., Inc.
Baltimore, Maryland
1995, 1998, 2000, 2002

International Standard Book Number: 0-8063-4570-5

Made in the United States of America

THE CONTRIBUTION OF NICHOLAS T. EKEL JR. WHO DEVELOPED

AND DONATED THE COMPUTER ASSISTED OUTLINE MAPS OF QUEBEC

IS GRATEFULLY ACKNOWLEDGED

CONTENTS

HOW TO USE THE PARISH GUIDE

The book is intended to help researchers locate their Catholic ancestors in Quebec, Canada.

Each county of the province has its own page. For each county there are references designed to help the researcher locate the county geographically, locate parishes within the county, locate the archives in which records for that county are housed and become aware of available published marriage registers. For the sake of this book, the counties of Jacques Cartier and Hochlega and the city of Montreal are referenced under the listing, I'lle Montreal. The county of Laval is found under the heading of I'lle Jesus. The Labrador peninsula is listed with the county of Saguenay.

On each county page, in addition to the name of the county, there is a map number referenced to the maps found in the front of the book, a notation whether the county is located north or south of the St. Lawrence river or on the Gaspe peninsula and a general reference indicating the location of the county in relationship to Quebec, Montreal, Ottawa or Three Rivers. The location of the archives which house early records for that county is given. A town, often the county town, located within the county is also listed.

Following these geographical references, the first parish organized within the county is listed, as well as the date when records of that parish are first found. Subsequent parishes in the county are listed in chronological order. All known Catholic parishes are listed to 1900, and a few beyond that date. A reference letter and name after the parish designates the compiler and publisher of a marriage repertoire for that parish. A list of publishers with reference letters is found near the front of the book An "L" after the parish name means that marriages for that parish are included in "Loiselles Marriage Index". A listing of the parishes indexed by Loiselle with dates is included within the reference section. There is, in addition to the parishes included in this reference, a supplement to the index which is not referenced. This supplement includes another 169,000 marriages of previously not included parishes. An "R" following the parish name designates inclusion in the "Rivest Marriage Index" as reported by the Allen County Public Library. The address for Rivest is included with the list of publishers. An * beside the county name means that there is a "whole county" repertoire of marriages published for that county. The reference is given at the bottom of the county page. An * beside a city means that there is an index published for all of the parishes in that city. Some protestant parishes and published marriage indexes are listed, but no attempt has been made to list all protestant parishes or protestant marriages indexes.

A listing of publishers and societies which publish parish records as well as their addresses is included in the first section of the book. When the address for a compiler or publisher is no longer current, an attempt has been made to list the current publisher.

1

Some repertoires are out of print and must be accessed through a library or through one of the regional archives in Quebec. Since the publishing of records is an ongoing project, failure of a parish to have a published repertoire referenced means only that knowledge of such a repertoire was not available at the time this book was written.

ADDITIONAL RESOURCES

INDEXES

Loiselle's Index to the Many Marriages of Quebec and Adjacent Areas was prepared by Pere Antonin Loiselle of the Convent des Dominicans, Montreal Quebec. It has been copied by the LDS church. There is also a supplement to the index which expands the index by 169,000 marriages.

The Rivest Index is a file of brides for the notarial districts of Joliette, St. Jerome, Mont Laurier and Sorel. It is available at the National Archives in Ottawa and at the regional archives in Montreal. The Fabien Marriage File covers the Outaouais, counties surrounding Montreal and Prince Edward Island. It is on microfilm and also available through the archives.

DROUIN

The Institut Genealogique Drouin at 2033 rue Sherbrooke Est Montreal, Quebec H2K 1C1 has published an extensive series of books indexing the marriages of the province of Quebec from 1750-1930. This series is in addition to the three volume set which contains some of the earliest marriages and bibliographies of pioneers of Quebec.

GUIDES

The archives nationales du Quebec at Ste. Foy has a computer diskette available for purchase which contains a complete list of the birth, death and marriage records held at the Archives Nationales du Quebec.

The Ottawa Branch of the Ontario Genealogical Society Box 8346 Ottawa, Ontario K1G 3H8 is in the process of compiling a current list of marriages repertoires held at the National Archives of Canada at Ottawa.

LIBRARIES

The central library of Montreal had an extensive collection of marriage repertoires. It is located at 1210 rue Sherbrooke Est Montreal, Quebec H2L 1L9. The librarians will respond to brief requests.

DATE VERIFICATION

All dates have been verified as follows:

Dates from 1621-1765 have been verified using:
Charbonneau, Hubert and Jacques Legare. _Le Repertoire des Actes de Bapteme, Mariage, Sepulture et des Recensements du Quebec Ancien._ Montreal: Presses de l'Universite de Montreal, 1980.

Dates from 1765-1876 have been verified using:
Belanger, Pauline and Yves Landry. _Inventaire Des Registres Paroissiaux Catholiques Du Quebec 1621-1876._ Montreal: Les Presses De l'Universite de Montreal, 1990.

Dates after 1876 have been verified as is possible using published marriage repertoires, materials from the regional archives, the Loiselle Marriage Index and an unpublished computerized reference from the Allen County Public Library in Ft. Wayne, Indiana.

Dates as listed are not necessarily the year of the formation of the parish, but rather the year in which records are first available for the parish.

If records for a parish are sometimes found with records of parishes located in a different county, then the parish is cross referenced for both counties. Some parishes have had name changes over time, an attempt has been made to include both names rather than to list them as two separate parishes. If a parish is listed in one of the references used, but it's existence cannot be verified, it has been listed with the referenced county.

Often dates vary with different references. For example: Belanger and Landry give the date of first records for St. Giles de Beaurivage in Lotbiniere county as 1829, while Pontbriand in his published marriage repertoire indicated that records began in 1843. Many discrepancies such as this have been noted. For the sake of consistency the verification policy given above has been followed. The researcher is encouraged to use all possible references in searching.

ARCHIVES

In addition to the national archives there are nine regional archives that house records over 100 years old. The archives contain copies of both protestant and catholic parish records. Many archives contain copies of the Loiselle, Rivest and Fabien marriage indexes. Copies of the 19th century censuses for the province of Quebec, notarial records, maps, judicial records, guides to land surveys, guides to Crown Land Grants and printed reference materials may also be found. Archives differ as to the availability of records as well as to records housed. It is best to contact the archives to ensure that materials are available. An attempt has been made to indicate for each county the branch of the regional archives where records for that county may be found.

Records less than 100 years old are housed at the Protonotaire's Office in the Palais de Justice of the local judicial district.

NATIONAL ARCHIVES

National Archives of Quebec
1210 Avenue du Seminaire
CP 10450
Sainte Foy, PQ G1V 4N1

REGIONAL ARCHIVES

Chicoutimi Regional Archives
930 rue Jacques-Cartier Est
Chicoutimi, PQ G7H 2A9

Hull Regional Archives
170 rue Hotel-de-Ville
Hull, PQ J8X 4C2

Montreal Regional Archives
1945 rue Mullins
Montreal, PQ H3K 1N9

Rimouski Regional Archives
337 rue Moreault
Rimouski, PQ G5L 1P4

Rouyn-Noranda Regional Archives
rue de Terminus Quest
Rouyn-Noranda, PQ J9X 2P3

Sept-Iles Regional Archives
649 boulevard Laure
Sept-Iles, PQ G4R 1X8

Sherbrooke Regional Archives

740 rue Galt Ouest
Sherbrooke, PQ   J1H   1Z3

Trois-Rivieres Regional Archives
225 rue des Forges
Trois-Rivieres, PQ   G9A   2G7

reference: Baxter, Angus. <u>In Search of Your Canadian Roots.</u>
Baltimore: Genealogical Publishing Co., Inc, 1989.

KEY TO QUEBEC COUNTY MAP

Abitibi	35	L'Islet	61
Argenteuil	22	Lotbiniere	53
Arthabaska	50	Maskinonge	27
Bagot	41	Matane	67
Beauce	58	Matapedia	66
Beauharnois	11	Megantic	54
Bellechasse	59	Missisquoi	40
Berthier	26	Montcalm	24
Bonaventure	70	Montmagny	60
Brome	43	Montmorency #1	32
Chambly	6	Montmorency #2	74
Champlain	29	Napierville	13
Charlevoix Est	37	Nicolet	49
Charlevoix Ouest	36	Papineau	20
Chateauguay	12	Pontiac	17
Chicoutimi	38	Portneuf	30
Compton	52	Quebec	31
Deux Montagnes	1	Richelieu	3
Dorchester	57	Richmond	46
Drummond	45	Rimouski	65
Frontenac	55	Riviere du Loup	63
Gaspe East	69	Rouville	7
Gaspe West	68	Saguenay	39
Gatineau	18	Shefford	42
Hull	19	Sherbrooke	47

Huntingdon	14	Soulanges	15
Iberville	8	Stanstead	48
I'le Jesus	71	St. Hyacinthe	5
I'le Montreal	72	St. Jean	9
Joliette	25	St. Maurice	28
Kamouraska	62	Temiscaminque	73
Labelle	21	Temiscouata	64
Lac St. Jean Est	33	Terrebonne	23
Lac St. Jean Ouest	34	Vaudreuil	16
Laprairie	10	Vercheres	4
L'Assomption	2	Wolfe	51
Levis	56	Yamaska	44

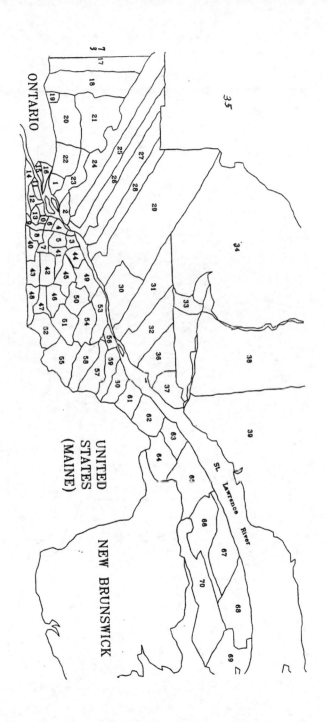

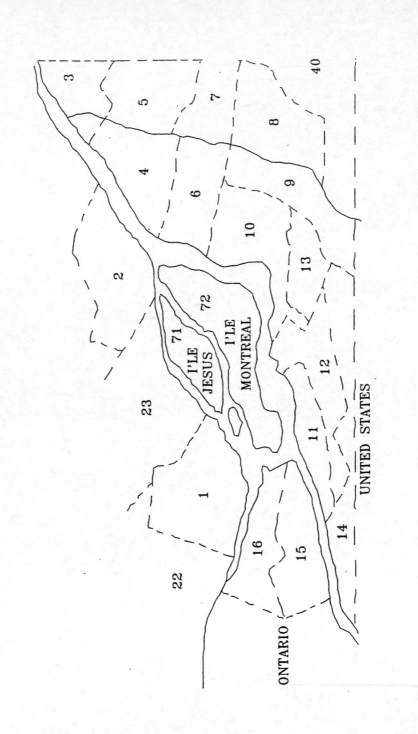

PARISH	COUNTY	DATES

Diocese Mt. Laurier

Cathedrale	Labelle	1894-1943
Ferme Neuve	Labelle	1901-1934
Gracefield	Gatineau	1867-1910
L'Assension	Labelle	1903-1925
Maniwaki	Gatineau	1851-1900
Nomininque	Labelle	1884-1926
Notre Dame de Laus	Labelle	1873-1900
St. Adolphe d'Howard	Argenteuil	1894-1900
Ste. Famile d'Aumond	Gatineau	1861-1942
St. Faustin	Terrebonne	1866-1950
Val Barrette	Labelle	1914-1944
Ville Marie	Temiscaminque	1880-1910

Diocese D'Ottawa

Basilique Notre Dame	Ottawa	1828-1840
St. Jean Bte d'Ottawa	Ottawa	1872-1886
Aylmer Est	Gatineau	1840-1864
Bourget	Russell Ont	1885-1906
Buckingham	Papineau	1836-1869
Clarence Creek	Ottawa	1855-1879
Grenville	Argenteuil	1839-1859
L'Original	Ottawa	1836-1880
Masson	Papineau	1886-1900
Notre Dame de la Salette	Papineau	1883-1900
Plantagenet	Ontario	1877-1880
St. Andre Avellin	Papineau	1855-1920
Ste. Anne	Prescott	1885-1951
Ste. Cecile	Prescott	1853-1896
St. Eugene	Prescott	1851-
St. Philip Argenteuil	Argenteuil	1856-1900
Ste. Rose de Lima	Papineau	1890-1930

Diocese Pembroke

Astorville	Nipissing	
Bonfield	Nipissing	
Corbeil	Nipissing	

Diocese Montreal

Notre Dame	I'le Montreal	1640-1840
Notre Dame de Grace	I'le Montreal	1867-1925
Sault au Recollet	I'le Montreal	1763-1860
Ile Bizard	I'le montreal	1843-1938
Lachenaie	L'Assomption	1683-1960
Lachine	I'le Montreal	1676-1879

Lachute	Argenteuil	1878-1900
L'Assomption	L'Assomption	1724-1960
Oka	Deux Montagnes	1721-1900
Pointe Aux Trembles	I'le Montreal	1674-1850
Pointe Claire	I'le Montreal	1713-1900
Repentigny	L'Assomption	1676-1900
Riviere des Praries	I'le Montreal	1688-1850
Ste. Adele	Terrebonne	1850-1900
St. Andre d'Argenteuil	Argenteuil	1833-1950
Carillon	Argenteuil	1918-1950
Ste. Anne de Bellevue	I'le Montreal	1703-1800
Ste. Anne des Plains	Terrebonne	1788-1900
St. Benoit	Deux Montagnes	1799-1900
St. Canut	Deux Montagnes	1858-1900
Ste. Dorothee	I'le Jesus	1869-1900
St. Eustache	Deux Montagnes	1769-1900
St. Francois de Sales	I'le Jesus	1702-1800
Ste. Genevieve	I'le Montreal	1741-1911
St. Hermos	Deux Montagnes	1837-1900
St. Hyppolite	Terrebonne	1867-1897
St. Janvier	Terrebonne	1845-1900
St. Jerome	Terrebonne	1832-1900
St. Joseph du Lac	Deux Montagnes	1855-1915
St. Laurent	I'le Montreal	1720-1939
St. Martin	I'le Jesus	1775-1850
St. Placide	Deux Montagnes	1850-1795
Ste. Rose de Laval	I'le Jesus	1745-1850
St. Sauveur	Terrebonne	1853-1900
Ste. Scholastique	Deux Montagnes	1825-1875
Ste. Sophie	Terrebonne	1706-1900
St. Sulpice	L'Assomption	1706-1949
Ste. Therese	Terrebonne	1789-1900
St. Vincent de Paul	I'le Jesus	1744-1899
Terrebonne	Terrebonne	1727-1900
Vaucluse		1903-1950

Diocese Joliette

Cathedrale	Joliette	1843-1905
Berthierville	Berthier	1727-1920
Ile Dupas	Berthier	1704-1900
Lanoraie	Berthier	1735-1900
Lavaltrie	Berthier	1716-1907
L'Epiphanie	L'Assomption	1857-1960
Mascouche	L'Assomption	1761-1900
Notre Dame de la Merci	Montcalm	1888-1920
Rawdon	Montcalm	1837-1925
St. Alexis Montcalm	Montcalm	1852-1900
St. Adolphe Rodriguez	Joliette	1843-1925
St. Ambroise de Kildare	Joliette	1832-1935
St. Barthelemy	Berthier	1828-1900
Ste. Beatrix	Joliette	1861-1910
St. Calixte de montcalm	Montcalm	1854-1947
St. Cleophas	Joliette	1897-1910
St. Come	Joliette	1867-1934

St. Cuthbert	Berthier	1765-1925
St. Edmond	Berthier	1889-1940
Ste. Elizabeth	Joliette	1802-1925
Ste. Emilie de l'Energie	Joliette	1870-1950
St. Esprit	Montcalm	1808-1900
St. Felix de Valois	Joliette	1843-1910
St. Gabriel de Brandon	Berthier	1840-1919
St. Jacques de Montcalm	Montcalm	1774-1960
St. Jean de Matha	Joliette	1855-1960
Ste. Julienne	Montcalm	1848-1920
St. Liguori	Montcalm	1848-1925
St. Lin	L'Assomption	1835-1909
Ste. Melanie	Joliette	1832-1900
St. Michel des Saints	Berthier	1864-1940
St. Norbert	Berthier	1849-1900
St. Paul	Joliette	1786-1940
St. Roch	L'Assomption	1787-1924
St. Theodore Chertsey	Montcalm	1856-1899
St. Thomas de Joliette	Joliette	1841-1906

Diocese Valleyfield

Beauharnois	Beauharnois	1819-1850
Chateauguay	Chateauguay	1736-1963
Howrick	Chateauguay	1863-1929
St. Antoine Abbe	Huntingdon	1860-1910
Ste. Barbe	Huntingdon	188201909
St. Clet	Soulanges	1849-1885
Ste. Clothilde	Chateauguay	1884-1923
Ste. Martine	Chateauguay	1823-1900
Ste. Philomene	Chateauguay	1840-1922
St. Polycarpe	Soulanges	1819-1879
St. Telesphore	Soulanges	1876-1900
St. Timothee	Beauharnois	1823-1920
St. Urbain	Chateauguay	1852-1869
Vaudreuil	Vaudreuil	1773-1847

Diocese St. Jean

Cathedrale	St. Jean	1828-1872
Boucherville	Chambly	1668-1908
Chambly	Chambly	1706-1944
Contrecoeur	Vercheres	1668-1920
L'Acadie	St. Jean	1784-1900
Laprarie	Laprairie	1667-1900
Napierville	Napierville	1823-1898
St. Bruno	Chambly	1843-1943
St. Constant	Laprairie	1752-1953
St. Isidore	Laprairie	1833-1943
St. Luc	St. Jean	1801-1885
St. Michel Archange	Napierville	1854-1944
St. Philippe	Laprairie	1751-1818
St. Valentin	St. Jean	1830-1856
Varennes	Vercheres	1693-1900
Vercheres	Vercheres	1709-1949

Diocese St. Hyacinthe

Cathedrale	St. Hyacinthe	1853-1950
Notre Dame du Rosarie	St. Hyacinthe	1777-1950
Christ-Roi	St. Hyacinthe	1927-1950
Providence	St. Hyacinthe	1937-1950
Abbotsford	Rouville	1855-1950
Acton Vale	Bagot	1858-1950
Adamsville	Brome	1872-1919
Bedford	Missisquoi	1869-1932
Clarenceville	Missisquoi	1872-1930
Ange Gardien	Rouville	1855-1950
Farnham	Missisquoi	1847-1900
Frelighsburg	Missisquoi	1866-1900
Notre Dame Granby	Shefford	1859-1915
Henryville	Iberville	1832-1900
Iberville	Iberville	1822-1911
LaPresentation	St. Hyacinthe	1806-1950
Marieville	Rouville	1801-1950
Milton	Shefford	1846-1900
Mont St. Gregorie	Iberville	1841-1900
Notre Dame Bonsecours Richelieu	Rouville	1860-1950
Rougemont	Rouville	1886-1950
Roxton Falls	Shefford	1850-1900
Roxton Pond	Shefford	1864-1900
St. Aime	Richelieu	1836-1900
St. Alexandre Iberville	Iberville	1850-1900
St. Adolphe Granby	Shefford	1869-1953
Ste. Angele de Monnoir	Rouville	1862-1950
Ste. Anne de Sorel	Richelieu	1876-1950
St. Antoine sur Richelieu	Vercheres	1750-1900
St. Barnabe Sud	St. Hyacinthe	1840-1950
Michaudville	St. Hyacinthe	1908-1950
Ste. Brigide Iberville	Iberville	1843-1900
St. Cesaire	Rouville	1822-1950
St. Charles sur Richelieu	St. Hyacinthe	1740-1950
St. Dennis sur Richelieu	St. Hyacinthe	1740-1950
St. Damase	St. Hyacinthe	1817-1950
St. Dominique de Bagot	Bagot	1823-1950
Ste. Helene de Bagot	Bagot	1853-1950
St. Hilaire	Rouville	1799-1950
St. Hugues	Bagot	1827-1950
St. Ignance de Stanbridge	Missisquoi	1876-1900
St. Jean Bte Rouville	Rouville	1797-1950
St. Jude	St. Hyacinthe	1822-1950
St. Liboire	Bagot	1856-1950
St. Louis de Bonsecours	Richelieu	1874-1940
Ste. Madeleine	Bagot	1876-1950
St. Marc	Vercheres	1792-1860
St. Marcel de Richelieu	Richelieu	1852-1950
St. Mathias	Rouville	1739-1950
St. Nazaire d'Acton	Bagot	1890-1950
St. Ours	Richelieu	1650-1888
St. Pie de Bagot	Bagot	1828-1950
St. Robert	Richelieu	1855-1906

St. Roch de Richelieu	Richelieu	1859-1900
Ste. Rosalie	Bagot	1832-1950
St. Simon	Bagot	1832-1950
St. Theodore d'ACton	Bagot	1841-1950
St. Thomas d'Acton	Compton	1889-1950
St. Valerien	Shefford	1854-1934
Ste. Victoire	Richelieu	1842-1938
St. Pierre Sorel	Richelieu	1642-1930
Upton	Bagot	1854-1950
Waterloo	Shefford	1865-1900

Diocese Sherbrooke

Cathedrale	Sherbrooke	1834-1900
St. Jean Bte	Sherbrooke	1884-1900
Christ Roi	Sherbrooke	1940-1947
Beebe	Stanstead	1925-1950
Bonsecours	Shefford	1840-1872
Bromptonville	Richmond	1885-1911
Chartierville	Compton	1878-1920
St. Edmond Coaticook	Stanstead	1868-1920
St. Jean Coaticook	Stanstead	1913-1940
St. Marc Coaticook	Stanstead	1917-1949
Compton	Compton	1855-1930
Katevale	Stanstead	1891-1930
Kingscroft	Stanstead	1901-1930
LaPatrie	Compton	1874-1905
Richmond	Richmond	1852-1866
Roc Forrest	Sherbrooke	1891-1920
Ste. Anne de Stukely	Shefford	1857-1939
St. Camille	Wolfe	1857-1900
Ste. Cecile de Frontenac	Frontenac	1887-1920
St. Elie d'Orford	Sherbrooke	1889-1920
Ste. Hedwige		1865-1920
St. Hermengilde	Stanstead	1875-1900
St. Julien	Wolfe	1864-1902
St. Malo	Compton	1883-1936
St. Romain	Compton	1865-1930
Scotstown	Compton	1888-1945
Stanstead	Stanstead	1848-1913
Stoke	Richmond	1872-1891
Stratford	Wolfe	1857-1900
Tres St. Enfant Jesus		1915-1936
Weedon	Wolfe	1866-1899
Wotton	Wolfe	1856-1900

Diocese Three Rivers

Cathedrale Trois Rivers	St. Maurice	1710-1870
Notre Dame Almaville	St. Maurice	1914-1936
Batiscan	Champlain	1682-1900
Cap de la Madeleine	Champlain	1687-1889
Champlain	Champlain	1679-1915
Shawinigan	St. Maurice	1900-1925
Louiseville	Maskinonge	1714-1900

Maskinonge	Maskinonge	1715-1900
Notre Dame de Mont Carmel	Champlain	1679-1915
Pointe de Lac	St. Maurice	1722-1900
St. Adolphe	Champlain	1889-1930
St. Alexis des Monts	Maskinonge	1871-1910
Ste. Anne de la Perade	Champlain	1693-1900
St. Didace	Maskinonge	1853-1874
Ste. Flore	St. Maurice	1864-1915
Ste. Genevieve de Batiscan	Champlain	1728-1900
St. Georges	Laviolette	1916-1930
St. Justin	Maskinonge	1858-1900
St. Leon	Maskinonge	1802-1900
St. Louis de France	Champlain	1903-1941
St. Prosper	Champlain	1856-1950
St. Severe	St. Maurice	1856-1905
St. Severin - Proulxville	Champlain	1888-1950
St. Stanislas	Champlain	1888-1900
St. Tite	Champlain	1859-1959
Yamachiche	St. Maurice	1718-1920

Diocese Nicolet

Cathedrale - Nicolet	Nicolet	1757-1930
Arthabaska	Arthabaska	1851-1900
Becancour	Nicolet	1722-
Gentilly	Nicolet	1784-1884
Kingsey	Drummond	1842-1900
LaBaie	Yamaska	1753-1869
L'Avenir	Drummond	1850-1930
Notre Dame de Pierreville	Yamaska	1894-1912
Notre Dame de Bon-Conseil	Drummond	1895-1940
Pierreville	Yamaska	1854-1939
Odanak	Yamaska	1940
Princeville	Arthabaska	1848-1850
St. Bonaventure	Yamaska	1886-1910
Ste. Brigitte	Nicolet	1863-1909
St. Celestin	Nicolet	1850-1881
Ste. Christine	Bagot	1888-1949
St. Cyril de Wendover	Drummond	1868-1930
St. David	Yamaska	1831-1950
St. Eugene de Grantham	Drummond	1878-1914
Ste. Eulalie	Nicolet	1871-1900
St. Francois du Lac	Yamaska	1715-1900
St. Fulgence de Durham	Drummond	1863-1930
St. Germain de Grantham	Drummond	1859-1900
Ste. Gertrude	Nicolet	1845-1890
St. Gregorie	Nicolet	1802-1900
St. Guillaume	Yamaska	1833-1900
St. Helene de Chester	Arthabaska	1869-1900
Ste. Monique	Nicolet	1842-1900
St. Norbert	Arthabaska	1845-1908
St. Paul de Chester	Arthabaska	1850-1900
Ste. Perpetue	Nicolet	1860-1935
St. Pie de Guire	Yamaska	1871-1910
St. Pierre les Becquets	Nicolet	1735-1900

St. Zephirin de Courval	Yamaska	1828-1900
Tingwick	Arthabaska	1857-1930
Ste Victoire - Victoriaville	Arthabaska	1865-1901
Warwick	Arthabaska	1858-1900
Wickham	Drummond	1864-1930
Yamaska	Yamaska	1731-1896

Diocese Quebec

Notre Dane de Quebec	Quebec	1755-1900
St. Jean Bte	Quebec	1886-1900
St. Roch	Quebec	1829-1900
St. Sauveur	Quebec	1853-1900
Stadacona	Quebec	1884-1920
Ancienne Lorette	Quebec	
Ange Gardien	Montmorency	1669-1920
Beauceville Ouest	Beauce	
Beaumont	Bellechasse	1850
Beauport	Quebec	1647-1900
Bergerville - Sillery	Quebec	1900
Breakeyville	Levis	1908-1930
Buckland	Bellechasse	1857-1929
Cap Rouge	Quebec	1862-1900
Cap St. Ignance	Montmagny	1670-1905
Cap Sante	Portneuf	1679-1948
Charlesbourg	Quebec	1759-1902
Charny	Levis	1902-1910
Chateau-Richer	Montmorency	1661-1902
Chaudiere Station	Levis	
Courcelles	Frontenac	1903-
Deschambault	Portneuf	1712-1940
Donnacona	Portneuf	1917-1939
Enfant Jesus	Beauce	1897-1940
Fortierville	Lotbiniere	1881-1932
Grondines	Portneuf	1680-1940
Grosse Ile	Montmagny	1834-1900
Ile aux Grues	Montmagny	1832-1921
Inverness	Megantic	1859-1940
Issoudun	Lotbiniere	1903-
Jeune Lorette	Quebec	1676-1915
Kamouraska	Kamouraska	1727-1900
Lac Noir	Megantic	1890-1904
Lambton	Frontenac	1844-1900
Langevin	Dorchester	1864-1920
Laurierville	Megantic	1852-1888
Lauzon	Levis	1685-1900
Laval	Montmorency	1849-1900
Les Ecureuils	Portneuf	1742-1940
Notre Dame Levis	Levis	1851-1909
L'Islet	L'Islet	1679-1875
Lotbiniere	Lotbiniere	1692-1920
Lyster	Megantic	1869-1910
Mont Carmel	Kamouraska	1859-1949
Montmagny	Montmagny	1678-1900
Neuville	Portneuf	1679-1940

19

Notre Dame de Lourdes	Megantic	1892-1930
Notre Dame de Portage	Riviere du Loup	185601900
Parisville	Lotbiniere	1920-1945
Plessisville	Megantic	1840-1876
Pont Rouge	Portneuf	1869-1930
Portneuf	Portneuf	1861-1939
St. Patrice	Riviere du Loup	1813-1900
St. Francois Xavier	Riviere du Loup	1905-1910
St. Adrien	Megantic	1879-1918
St. Agapit	Lotbiniere	1868-
Ste. Agathe	Lotbiniere	1853-1873
St. Alban	Portneuf	1856-1908
St. Alexandre	Kamouraska	1850-1920
St. Andre	Kamouraska	1791-1896
Ste. Anne de Beaupre	Montmorency	1657-1914
Ste. Anne de la Pocatiere	Kamouraska	1715-1950
St. Antoine de Tilly	Lotbiniere	1702-1946
St. Antonin	Kamouraska	1856-1900
St. Appolinaire	Lotbiniere	1857-1920
St. Aubert	L'Islet	1858-1922
St. Augustin	Portneuf	1691-1920
St. Basile	Portneuf	1847-1946
St. Casmir	Portneuf	1847-1913
St. Charles	Bellechasse	1749-1927
Ste. Catherine	Portneuf	1832-1944
Ste. Croix	Lotbiniere	1716-1946
St. Cyrille	L'Islet	1844-1901
St. David	Levis	1877-1907
St. Denis	Kamouraska	1841-1949
St. Edouard	Lotbiniere	1868-1910
St. Eleuthere	Kamouraska	1874-1905
Ste. Emilie	Lotbiniere	1862-1947
St. Etienne de Lauzon	Levis	1861-1909
St. Eugene	L'Islet	1874-1944
St. Evariste	Frontenac	1855-1900
Ste. Famile I.O.	Montmorency #2	1661-1920
St. Ferdinand	Megantic	1847-1931
St. Ferreol	Montmorency	1810-1900
St. Flavien	Lotbiniere	185601920
Ste. Foye	Quebec	1698-1900
St. Francois I.O	Montmorency #2	1679-1904
St. Frederic	Beauce	1851-1900
St. Gervais	Bellechasse	1780-1890
St. Gilbert	Portneuf	1893-1919
St. Gilles	Lotbiniere	1830-1908
St. Gregorie	Montmorency	1890-1919
Ste. Helene	Kamouraska	1855-1900
St. Henri	Levis	1780-1900
St. Honore	Beauce	1873-1900
St. Jean Chysostome	Levis	1830-1909
St. Deschaillons	Lotbiniere	1744-1870
St. Jean I.O.	Montmorency #2	1679-1927
St. Jean Port Joly	L'Islet	1767-1826
St. Joachim	Montmorency	1687-1909
St. Lambert	Levis	1854-1911

St. Laurent I.O.	Montmorency #2	1679-1910
St. Lazare	Bellechasse	1856-1940
St. Leonard	Portneuf	1897-1932
St. Magloire	Bellechasse	1856-1916
Ste. Marguerite	Dorchester	1840-1900
Ste. Marie	Beauce	1745-
St. Methode	Frontenac	1889-1930
St. Michel	Bellechasse	1693-1904
St. Narcisse	Lotbiniere	1873-1920
St. Nicholas	Levis	1694-1946
St. Octave - Dosquet	Lotbiniere	1912-1944
St. Pacome	Kamouraska	1853-1900
St. Patrice	Lotbiniere	1871-1946
St. Paul de montmagny	Montmagny	1868-1920
Ste. Petronille I.O.	Montmorency #2	1872-1935
St. Philemon	Bellechasse	1886-1925
St. Philippe de Nery	Kamouraska	1870-1930
St. Pierre I.O.	Montmorency #2	1679-1902
St. Raymond	Portneuf	1844-1960
St. Roch des Aulnaies	L'Islet	1735-1861
St. Romuald	Levis	1855-1861
Ste. Sabine	Bellechasse	1906-1930
St. Samuel	Frontenac	1872-1920
St. Sebastien	Frontenac	1869-1920
Ste. Sophie	Megantic	1855-1898
St. Sylvestre	Lotbiniere	1829-1900
St. Tite des Caps	Montmorency	1858-1913
St. Ubald	Portneuf	1860-1908
St. Valier	Bellechasse	1713-1925
Stoneham	Quebec	1870-1900
Valcartier	Quebec	1843-1900
Villeroy	Lotbiniere	1910-1924

Diocese Chicoutimi

Cathedrale	Chicoutimi	1845-1870
Bagotville	Chicoutimi	1847-1870
Hebertville	Lac St. Jean	1852-1903
St. Dominique de Jonquiere	Chicoutimi	1866-1934
Grande Baie	Chicoutimi	1842-1914
Laterriere	Chicoutimi	1851-1902
Metabetchouan	Lac St. Jean	1869-1900
Notre Dame du Lac - Roberval	Lac St. Jean	1862-1900
Ste. Anne de Chicoutimi	Chicoutimi	1861-1920
St. Honore	Chicoutimi	1910-1923

Diocese Gaspe

Cloridorme	Gaspe Nord
Grande Vallee	Gaspe Nord
Newport	Gaspe Sud
Paspebiac	Bonaventure
Port Daniel est	Bonaventure
Riviere au Renard	Gaspe Sud

Diocese d'Amos

Palmorolle	1935–1955
Taschereau	1915–1938

QUEBEC PUBLISHERS AND GENEALOGICAL SOCIETIES

A.   Ghislaine M. Beaulieu
701 rue Simard
Roberval, Quebec   G8h   1T4

B.   F. Dominique Campagna   (through LeCentre de Genealogie)
Pavillon Andre-Coindre
Cap Rouge, Quebec   G0A   1K0

C.   Editions Bergeron Inc.
C.P. 812 St. Germain
Grantham, Quebec J0C   1K0

D.   Editions Elysee
C.P. 188   Succursale Cote St. Luc
Montreal, Quebec   H4V   2Y4

E.   La Societe de Genealogie de l'Outaouais Inc.
C.P. 2025 succ "B"
Hull, Quebec   J8X   3Z2

F.   Le Centre De Genealogie S.C.
2244 Rue Fullum
Montreal, Quebec   H2K   3N9

G.   LaSociete d'Histoire de la Seigneurie de Chambly
CP 142
Chambly, Quebec   J3L   4B1

H.   Les Editions du Pre. Leger (address not current)
303 Boul. du Havre
Salaberry de Valleyfield, Quebec S6S   1S5

I.   Mme. Francine Perrault-Forest
922 Boul. Manseau
Joliette, Quebec   J6E 3G5

J.   M. Benoit Pontbriand
2390 Marie-Victorin
Sillery, Quebec   G1T   1K1

K.   Societe Canadienne de Genealogie
(try Societe de Genealogie de Quebec)
C.P. 2234
Quebec, 2e Quebec Canada

L.   Societe Genealogique Canadienne Francaise
CP 335   Station Place D'Armes
Montreal, Quebec   H2Y   3H1

M.   Societe De Genealogie Des Cantons de l'Est

23

CP 635
Sherbrooke, Quebec J1H 5K5

N. Societe Genealogique de l'Est du Quebec
CP 253
Rimouski, Quebec G5L 7C1

O. Societe de Genealogie de la Maurice et Bois Francs
CP 901
Trois Rivieres, Quebec G9A 5K2

P. Societe de Genealogie de Quebec
CP 9066 (1210 Avenue du Seminaire)
Sainte Foy, Quebec G1V 4A8

Q. La Societe Genealogie de Lanaudiere
CP 221
Joliette, Quebec J6E 3Z6

R. M. Armand Proulx (through Societe de Genealogie de Quebec)
CP 636 (1015 6E Avenue)
LaPocatiere, Quebec G0R 1Z0

S. Societe d'Historire et de Genealogie Matane
145 rue Soucy
Matane, Quebec G4W 2E1

T. Societe Genealogie des Laurentides
CP 131
St. Jerome, Quebec J7Z 5T7

U. Societe French Ontario History

V. Lost In Canada (Minnesota Genealogical Society)
P.O. Box 16069
St. Paul, Mn. 55116

W. McDonald Research Center
268 Bartholomew St.
OntarioBrockville, Ontario K6V 2S6

X. La Societe Genealogique du Saguenay
through Societe de Genealogique de Quebec
CP 814
Chicoutimi, Quebec G7H 5E8

Y. American French Genealogical Society
PO Box 2113
Pawtucket, RI 02861-0113

Z. Society History de St. Nicholas & Berniers

AA.   Centre de Genealogie Madeleine Inc. (Musee de la Mer)
CP 69
Havre-Aubert, Iles de la Madeleine G0B 1J0

BB.   Federation Quebecoise des Societes de Genealogie
CP 9454
Ste. Foy. Quebec G1V 4B8

CC.   Quebec Family History Society
CP 1026
Pointe Claire, Quebec H9S 4H9

DD.   Societe de Genealogie de la Cote-Nord
649 Boul. Laure
Sept-Iles, Quebec G4R 1X8

EE.   Societe de Genealogie Salaberry de Valleyfield
CP 164
Valleyfield, Quebec J6S 2M2

FF.   Societe d'Historie et de Genealogie de Dolbeau
(Societe Genealogie Saguenay)
CP 201
Dolbeau, Quebec G8L 2R1

GG.   Societe d'Histoire et d'Archeologie des Monts
CP 1192
Ste. Anne des Monts, Gaspesie G0E 2G0

HH.   Societe d'Historie et de Genealogie de la Matapedia
CP 1737
Amqui, Quebec G0J 1B0

II.   Societe d'Historie et de Genealogie de Riviere du Loup
65 rue Hotel de Ville
Riviere du Loup, Quebec G5R 1L4

JJ.   Societe d'Historie et de Genealogie de St. Prosper
CP 39
St. Prosper, Quebec G0X 3A0

KK.   Societe du Patrimoine et de Genealogie de Rouyn-Noranda
541 ave Laliberte
Rouyn-Noranda, Quebec J9X 3X7

LL.   Societe du Patrimoine et de Genealogie du Canton Nedelec
CP 186
Notre Dame du Nord, Quebec J0Z 3B0

MM.   Societe Genealogie de la Presqu'ile
137 rue Ste. Catherine
St. Polycarpe, Quebec J0P 1X0

NN.   Societe Genealogique de la Region de l'Amiante
671 Boul. Smith Sud
Thetford Mines, Quebec G6G 1N1

OO.   Societe Genealogie de Montmagny (address not current)
188 rue St. Ignance
Montmagny, Quebec H2T 2Y1

PP.   Societe Genealogie du K.R.T - Presbytere de St. Epiphane
(through Societe Genealogie de Quebec)
CP 87 (258 ave Sirois)
St. Epiphane, Quebec GOL 2X0

QQ.   Societe Historique et Genealogique de Ste. Julienne
CP 429 (2482 Place Rivet)
Ste. Julienne, Quebec J0K 2T0

RR.   Societe Historique et Genealogique de Trois Pistoles
J. Francois Beaulieu
CP 1478
Trois-Pistoles, Quebec GOL 4K0

SS.   Societe Monteregienne de Genealogie
251 rue Beique
Chambly, Quebec J3L 1H1

TT.   Rivest (address not current)
1145 St. Viateur
Outremont, Montreal, Quebec

UU.   Rosaire St. Pierre
135 Rue du Domaine
Beaumont, Bellechasse Quebec
GOR   1C0

VV.   Robert-Edmond Gingras (address not current)
2360 Chemin
Ste. Foye, Quebec
10 P Q

XX.   Publisher Unknown

COUNTY: Abitibi *

LOCATION: Far North

REFERENCE: North of Ottawa

MAP: 35

ARCHIVES: Rouyn-Noranda

CITY REFERENCE: Amos

FIRST PARISH: 1893 - Mistassini - (James Bay) - see Lac St. Jean
Quest

PARISH: 1913 - Cathedrale Ste Therese (Amos) - east

PARISH: 1914 - St. Pierre (Taschereau) - west L

PARISH: 1917 - St. Philippe (La Reine) - west

PARISH: 1917 - St. Andre (La Sarre) - west XX-Leboeuf & Bussiere

PARISH: 1917 - St. Jean l'Evangeliste (Macimic)- west

PARISH: 1918 - St. Jacques Le Majeur (Barraute) - east

PARISH: 1918 - St. Luc (La Motte) - east

PARISH: 1918 - St. Barnabe (Landrienne) - east

PARISH: 1918 - St. Paul (Senneterre) - east

PARISH: 1919 - St. Simon (Vilemontel) - east

PARISH: 1919 - St. Jude (Authier) - west

PARISH: 1919 - St. Jacques Le Mineur (Dupuy) - west

*M-Collaboration - west includes Baie James (Mistassini)
east - 2 volumes

COUNTY: Argenteuil *

LOCATION: North

REFERENCE: Northwest of Montreal

MAP: 22

ARCHIVES: Montreal

CITY REFERENCE: Lachute

FIRST PARISH: 1805 - Chatham - (Protestant)

PARISH: 1812 - St. Andrews East - (Protestant)

PARISH: 1833 - St. Andre d'Argenteuil L R T-Collaboration

PARISH: 1837 - Dalesville - (Protestant)

PARISH: 1839 - Notre Dame de Sept Douleurs - (Mission de
Grenville) L R T-Collaboration (Vol4)

PARISH: 1846 - Ste Anne du Grand Calumet - see Pontiac

PARISH: 1856 - St. Philippe de Argenteuil (Chatham)
L R T-Collaboration (Vol3)

PARISH: 1878 - Ste Anastasie (Lachute) L R
T-Collaboration (Vol2)

PARISH: 1882 - Pointe aux Chenes R T-Collaboration (Vol4)

PARISH: 1882 - St. Adolphe de Howard L R T-Collaboration (Vol1)

PARISH: 1884 - Montfort R T-Collaboration (Vol1)

PARISH: 1887 - Notre Dame de la Merci - (Huberdeau) R
T-Collaboration (Vol1)

PARISH: 1889 - St. Michel de Wentworth R T-Collaboration (Vol3)

* - TT. - Rivest

COUNTY: Arthabaska *

LOCATION: South

REFERENCE: Southeast of Three Rivers

MAP: 50

ARCHIVES: Three Rivers

CITY REFERENCE: Arthabaska

FIRST PARISH: 1845 - St. Norbert (Norbertville) L

PARISH: 1848 - St. Eusebe de Stanfold (Princeville) L
                J-Bergeron

PARISH: 1848 - St. Louis de Blandford

PARISH: 1852 - St. Christophe L

PARISH: 1857 - St. Patrice de Tingwick L J-Pontbriand

PARISH: 1858 - St. Medard de Warwick L

PARISH: 1860 - St. Paul de Chester L F-Campagna

PARISH: 1861 - St. Valere de Bulstrode

PARISH: 1865 - Ste. Victorie (Victoriaville) L

PARISH: 1868 - Ste. Clothilde de Horton J-Laliberte & Pontbriand

PARISH: 1869 - Ste. Helene de Chester L

PARISH: 1875 - St. Aime de Kingsey Falls - see Drummond

PARISH: 1876 - St. Albert de Warwick

PARISH: 1880 - Ste. Elizabeth de Warwick

PARISH: 1881 - St. Remi de Tingwick

PARISH: 1888 - Ste. Anne de Sault (Daveluyville)

PARISH: 1893 - St. Rosarie

* M-Collaboration (2 Volumes + supplement)
* F-Campagna
* L-Fabien

COUNTY: Bagot *

LOCATION: South

REFERENCE: Southwest of Three Rivers

MAP: 41

ARCHIVES: Sherbrooke

CITY REFERENCE: St. Liboire

FIRST PARISH: 1827 - St. Hugues L J-Pontbriand & Jette

PARISH: 1830 - St. Pie L XX-Delorme F-Collaboration (1901-1988)

PARISH: 1832 - St. Simon (St. Simon de Ramsay) L J-Pontbriand
              & Jette

PARISH: 1834 - Ste. Rosalie L

PARISH: 1837 - St. Dominique L

PARISH: 1854 - Ste. Helene L J-Pontbriand & Jette

PARISH: 1856 - St. Ephrem d'Upton L J-Pontbriand & Jette

PARISH: 1858 - St. Andre de Acton (Acton Vale) L
              J-Pontbriand & Jette

PARISH: 1859 - St. Liboire de Ramezay L

PARISH: 1862 - St. Theodore d'Acton L J-Pontbriand & Jette

PARISH: 1876 - Ste. Marie Madeleine - see St. Hyacinthe

PARISH: 1886 - Ste. Christine L J-Pontbriand & Jette

PARISH: 1890 - St. Nazaire d' Acton L J-Pontbriand & Jette

* J-Pontbriand & Jette

COUNTY: Beauce *

LOCATION: South

REFERENCE: South of Quebec near Maine

MAP: 58

ARCHIVES: Quebec

CITY REFERENCE: Beauceville

FIRST PARISH: 1739 - St. Joseph de Nouvelle Beauce

PARISH: 1745 - Ste. Marie de Nouvelle Beauce L

PARISH: 1765 - St. Francois d'Assise de la Nouvelle Beauce
         (Beauceville) L P-Gilbert Leveille

PARISH: 1841 - St. Georges d'Aubert Gallion

PARISH: 1846 - St. Elzear de Liniere

PARISH: 1848 - St. Vital de Lambton L

PARISH: 1848 - St. Victor de Tring

PARISH: 1852 - St. Frederic L

PARISH: 1855 - St. Evariste de Forsyth L

PARISH: 1855 - St. Pierre de Broughton

PARISH: 1866 - St. Ephrem de Tring NN-Collaboration

PARISH: 1869 - St. Sebastien de Lambton L

PARISH: 1871 - Sacre Coeur de Jesus (East Broughton) P-Grouleau

PARISH: 1871 - St. Come de Kennebec (Liniere) P-Beaudoin

PARISH: 1872 - St. Severin

PARISH: 1873 - St. Honore de Shenley L

PARISH: 1875 - Sts. Anges

PARISH: 1881 - St. Zacharie

PARISH: 1882 - St. Martin

PARISH: 1891 - St. Theophile

PARISH: 1892 - St. Benoit Labre

PARISH: 1897 - Enfant Jesus   L

PARISH: 1899 - St. Gedeon

* L-Frere Eloi-Gerard Talbot
  Q-Eloi-Gerard Talbot (11 Volumes Beauce, Dorchester & Frontenac)

COUNTY: Beauharnois

LOCATION: South

REFERENCE: Southwest of Montreal

MAP: 11

ARCHIVES: Montreal (1855 Valleyfield Diocese)

CITY REFERENCE: Salaberry de Valleyfield *

FIRST PARISH: 1819 - St. Clement L R F-Charette

PARISH: 1823 - St. Timothee L F-Charette

PARISH: 1847 - St. Louis de Gonzague F-Charette

PARISH: 1858 - Ste. Cecile (Valleyfield)

PARISH: 1859 - St. Stanislas de Kostka F-Campagna F-Charette

PARISH: 1866 - Ste Agnes de Dundee (Valleyfield) - see Huntingdon

PARISH: 1869 - St. Etienne H-Leger & Pregent

PARISH: 1900 - Notre Dame de Bellerive (L'Immaculee Conception)
              (Valleyfield) H-Leger & Pregent

PARISH: 1928 - Sacre Coeur de Jesus (Valleyfield)

*Diocese of Valleyfield F-Charette

COUNTY: Bellechasse *

LOCATION: South

REFERENCE: Southeast of Quebec

MAP: 59

ARCHIVES: Quebec

CITY REFERENCE: St. Raphael

FIRST PARISH: 1692 - St. Etienne de Beaumont   L   C-St.Pierre

PARISH: 1693 - St. Michel de la Durantaye   L   C-Goulet (deaths)
XX-Turgeon

PARISH: 1713 - St. Vallier   L

PARISH: 1749 - St. Charles de Bellechasse   (St. Charles de
Beaumont) (St.Charles Borromee)   L   C-Goulet

PARISH: 1780 - Sts. Gervais et Protais   L   C-Goulet

PARISH: 1849 - St. Lazare   L   C-Goulet

PARISH: 1851 - St. Raphael   C-Goulet

PARISH: 1857 - St. Cajetan d'Armagh   C-Goulet

PARISH: 1857 - Notre Dame Auxiliatrice des Montagnes de Buckland
L   C-Goulet

PARISH: 1872 - St. Magloire de Roux   L   C-Goulet

PARISH: 1882 - St. Damien   C-Goulet

PARISH: 1883 - St. Neree   C-Goulet

PARISH: 1886 - St. Philemon   L   C-Goulet

* C-St. Pierre, Rosaire
  Q - Eloi-Gerard Talbot   16 Volumes (Montmagny, L'Islet,
      Bellechasse)

34

COUNTY: Berthier *

LOCATION: North

REFERENCE: East of Montreal

MAP: 26

ARCHIVES: Montreal

CITY REFERENCE: Berthierville

FIRST PARISH: 1727 - La Visitation de la Sainte Vierge Marie
(I'le Dupas) L R F-Campagna & Rivest
Q-Goyette

PARISH: 1727 - Ste. Genevieve de Berthier en Haut (Berthierville)
L R F-Campagna & Rivest

PARISH: 1732 - St. Joseph de Lanoraie L R I-Dufresne

PARISH: 1737 - St. Antoine de Lavaltrie (St. Antoine de Pade) L
R C-Collaboration, F-Campagna, Q-Laporte

PARISH: 1770 - St. Cuthbert (Chicot) L R Q-Dufresne

PARISH: 1828 - St. Barthelemy L R

PARISH: 1832 - Ste. Melanie d'Ailleboust - see Joliette

PARISH: 1839 - St. Gabriel de Brandon (Lac Maskinonge) L R
Q-Gravel Q-Beausoleil

PARISH: 1847 - St. Norbert L R Q-Lambert

PARISH: 1864 - St. Michel des Saints L R Q-LaSalle-Beausejour
F-Collaboration

PARISH: 1867 - St. Damien de Brandon R

PARISH: 1886 - St. Zenon R Q-LaSalle-Beausejour

PARISH: 1889 - St. Edmond L R Q-Coutu

PARISH: 1895 - I'le St. Ignance de Loyola R F-Campagna

* TT.- Rivest (4 Volumes)

COUNTY: Bonaventure *

LOCATION: Gaspe (La Gaspesie)

REFERENCE: Southern Gaspe, North of New Brunswick
(Bay of Chaleurs)

MAP: 70

ARCHIVES: Rimouski

CITY REFERENCE: New Carlisle

FIRST PARISH: 1759 - Ste. Anne de Ristigouche (Cross Point)

PARISH: 1791 - St. Bonaventure de Bonaventure

PARISH: 1795 - St. Joseph de Carleton (Tracadieche) (Baie des
Chaleurs) **Arsenault

PARISH: 1826 - Notre Dame de la Purification (Paspebiac)
L **Arsenault

PARISH: 1831 - Sts. Anges Gardiens de Cascapediac (New Richmond)
**Arsenault

PARISH: 1855 - St. Georges de Port Daniel (Notre Dame du Mt.
Carmel) L **Arsenault

PARISH: 1859 - St. James (Port Daniel) **Arsenault

PARISH: 1860 - Ste. Brigitte de Maria **Arsenault

PARISH: 1865 - St. Bonaventure de Hamilton **Arsenault

PARISH: 1867 - St. Charles de Caplan **Arsenault

PARISH: 1869 - St. Jean l'Evangeliste (Nouvelle) **Arsenault

PARISH: 1871 - St. Alexis - see Matapedia

PARISH: 1875 - St. Godefroi **Arsenault

PARISH: 1884 - Mission de Causapscal - see Matapedia

PARISH: 1899 - St. Omer **Arsenault

* Arsenault - Editions Marquis

** Chau T.V.
Television de la Baie des Chaleurs
C.P. 100
Carleton, Quebec G0C 1J0

COUNTY: Brome *

LOCATION: Far South

REFERENCE: South of Three Rivers near Vermont

MAP: 43

ARCHIVES: Sherbrooke

CITY REFERENCE: Knowlton

FIRST PARISH: 1841 - Mission des Cantons L'Est - see Shefford

PARISH: 1851 - St. Etienne Bolton

PARISH: 1866 - St. Andre de Sutton

PARISH: 1868 - St. Edouard de Brome (Knowlton)

PARISH: 1873 - St. Vincent Ferrier (Adamsville) L

PARISH: 1876 - St. Rose de Lima (Cowansville) - see Missisquoi

PARISH: 1881 - St. Cajetan (Mansonville)

PARISH: 1894 - St. Edouard (Eastman)

PARISH: 1914 - St. Benoit de Lac

* J- R.Jette & Beauregard

COUNTY: Chambly *

LOCATION: South

REFERENCE: South of Montreal

MAP: 6

ARCHIVES: Montreal

CITY REFERENCE: Longueuil

FIRST PARISH: 1668 - Ste. Famille de Boucherville L J-Pontbriand
                     J-Rivet (1901-1970)

PARISH: 1699 - St. Antoine de Pade de Longueuil C-Gareau

PARISH: 1706 - St. Joseph de Chambly L J-Jette

PARISH: 1843 - St. Bruno de Montarville L J-Jette

PARISH: 1862 - St. Hubert G-Rivet

PARISH: 1871 - St. Basile le Grand J-Jette

PARISH: 1895 - St. Lambert G-Rivet XX-Talbot

* G-Rivet (1862-1972)

COUNTY: Champlain

LOCATION: North

REFERENCE: East of Three Rivers

MAP: 29

ARCHIVES: Three Rivers

CITY REFERENCE: Cap de la Madeleine

FIRST PARISH: 1673 - Ste Marie Madeleine du Cap de la Madeleine
L F-Campagna, O-Collaboration, K-Roberge

PARISH: 1679 - St. Francois Xavier de Batiscan L F-Campagna

PARISH: 1679 - Notre Dame de la Visitation (La Visitation de
Champlain) L F-Campagna O-Collaboration (2
Volumes)

PARISH: 1679 - Ste Anne de la Perade L F-Campagna

PARISH: 1727 - Ste Genevieve de Batiscan L F-Campagna

PARISH: 1787 - St. Stanislas de la Riviere des Envies L
F-Campagna, O-Lacoursiere (deaths)

PARISH: 1844 - St. Maurice C-Daneau

PARISH: 1849 - St. Prosper L F-Campagna JJ-Collaboration

PARISH: 1854 - St. Narcisse F-Campagna

PARISH: 1859 - St. Tite L F-Campagna

PARISH: 1863 - St. Luc de Vincennes F-Campagna

PARISH: 1864 - Notre Dame du Mt. Carmel (Valmont) L

PARISH: 1865 - Ste Flore (Grand Mere) L C-Lesieur

PARISH: 1878 - St. Theodore (Grand 'Anse)

PARISH: 1880 - St. Thecle (Lac Aux Chicots)
XX-Beland, Veilette et al)

PARISH: 1888 - St. Severe de Proulxville L

PARISH: 1890 - St. Adelphe L

PARISH: 1890 - Riviere au Rat (Grand 'Anse) F-Collaboration

PARISH: 1984 - St. Georges

PARISH: 1894 - St. Theophile du Lac (Lac a la Tortue)
                  O-Collaboration

PARISH: 1898 - St. Timothee d'Herouxville

PARISH: 1899 - St. Paul de Grand Mere F-Lesieur

PARISH: 1899 - St. Zephirin (La Tuque) F-Lessard

PARISH: 1902 - St. Louis de France L O-Collaboration

COUNTY: Charlevoix Est *

LOCATION: North

REFERENCE: Northeast of Quebec

MAP: 37

ARCHIVES: Quebec/Chicoutimi

CITY REFERENCE: La Malbaie

FIRST PARISH: 1774 - St. Etienne de La Malbaie

PARISH: 1833 - Ste. Agnes - La Malbaie

PARISH: 1843 - St. Irenee

PARISH: 1855 - St. Fidele de Mont Murray

PARISH: 1874 - St. Simeon

* X- Talbot (5 Volume Genealogy)
   P- Anctil-Tremblay (3 Volumes)

COUNTY: Charlevoix Quest   *

LOCATION: North

REFERENCE: Northeast of Quebec

MAP: 36

ARCHIVES: Quebec/Chicoutimi

CITY REFERENCE: Baie St. Paul

FIRST PARISH: 1681 - St. Pierre & St. Paul de Baie St. Paul

PARISH: 1734 - St. Francois-Xavier de Petite Riviere

PARISH: 1734 - L'Assomption de la Ste. Vierge des Eboulements
                  (Notre Dame des Eboulements) P-Anctil-Tremblay

PARISH: 1741 - St. Louis de Isle Aux Coudres

PARISH: 1827 - St. Urbain

PARISH: 1864 - St. Hilarion de Settrington

PARISH: 1884 - St. Placide

* X- Talbot (5 Volume Genealogy)
  P- Anctil-Tremblay (3 Volumes)

COUNTY: Chateauguay *

LOCATION: South

REFERENCE: Near New York

MAP: 12

ARCHIVES: Montreal

CITY REFERENCE: Ste. Martine

FIRST PARISH: 1736 - St. Joachim de Chateauguay   (Mission Sault
                     St. Louis) L L-Julien

PARISH: 1823 - Ste. Martine L C-Boulianne

PARISH: 1838 - St. Chrysostome (St. Jean Chrysostome)
               XX-Pregent   V-Reisinger

PARISH: 1840 - Ste. Philomene (Ville Mercier) L

PARISH: 1846 - St. Malachie d'Ormstown

PARISH: 1852 - St. Urbain Premier L

PARISH: 1860 - St. Antoine Abbe - see Huntingdon

PARISH: 1863 - Tres Saint Sacrement (Howick) L

PARISH: 1885 - Ste. Clothilde L C-Roy

* C-Roy

COUNTY: Chicoutimi *

LOCATION: Far North

REFERENCE: Northwest of Quebec

MAP: 38

ARCHIVES: Chicoutimi

CITY REFERENCE: Chicoutimi

FIRST PARISH: 1842 - St. Alexis de Grande Baie (La Baie)
                      (Port Alfred) L XX-Gareau
                      O-Gagne XX-Belanger

PARISH: 1845 - St. Francois Xavier de Chicoutimi (Cathedrale) L
               XX-Belanger

PARISH: 1852 - Notre Dame d'Hebertville - see Lac St. Jean Est

PARISH: 1855 - Notre Dame de L'Immaculee Conception
               de Laterriere L XX-Belanger

PARISH: 1858 - St. Alphonse de Ligouri de la Grande Baie
               (Bagotville) L O-Gagne XX-Belanger

PARISH: 1860 - Ste. Anne de Saguenay (Chicoutimi Nord) L
               XX-Belanger

PARISH: 1860 - Notre Dame du Lac (Roberval) - see Lac St. Jean
               Ouest

PARISH: 1861 - St. Jean Bte d L'Anse St. Jean - see Lac St. Jean
               Ouest

PARISH: 1866 - St. Dominique de Jonquiere L

PARISH: 1869 - St. Jerome du Lac St. Jean - see Lac St. Jean Est

PARISH: 1871 - St. Fulgence de l'Anse aux Foins O-Poulin

PARISH: 1872 - St. Prime - see Lac St. Jean Quest

PARISH: 1872 - St. Louis de Metabetchouan (Chambord) - see
               Lac St. Jean Est

PARISH: 1910 - St. Honore L

PARISH: 1932 - Ste. Rose du Nord O-Poulin

PARISH: 1935 - Ste. Bernadette de Boileau

* XX-Gosselin

COUNTY: Compton *

LOCATION: Far South

REFERENCE: South of Quebec near New Hampshire

MAP: 52

ARCHIVES: Sherbrooke

CITY REFERENCE: Cookshire

FIRST PARISH: 1855 - St. Thomas d'Aquin (Compton) L

PARISH: 1862 - St. Venant de Hereford (Paquetteville)

PARISH: 1865 - St. Romain de Winslow - see Frontenac

PARISH: 1868 - St. Camille de Cookshire (Lellis)

PARISH: 1868 - St. Raphael de Bury

PARISH: 1873 - St. Pierre de Ditton (La Patrie) L

PARISH: 1873 - Ste. Edwidge de Clifton

PARISH: 1883 - La Decollation de St. Jean Baptiste (Chartierville) L

PARISH: 1884 - St. Malo L

PARISH: 1888 - St. Louis de France (East Angus)

PARISH: 1888 - St. Paul (Scotstown) L

PARISH: 1894 - Notre Dame du St. Rosarie (Sawyerville)

PARISH: 1906 - St. Martin (Martinville)

PARISH: 1907 - St. Henri (East Hereford)

PARISH: 1907 - Assomption de la Bienheureuse Vierge Marie (Waterville)

* M-Collaboration (2 Volumes)
  F-Campagna

COUNTY: Deux Montagnes **

LOCATION: North

REFERENCE: North of Montreal

MAP: 1

ARCHIVES: Montreal

CITY REFERENCE: Ste. Scholastique

FIRST PARISH: 1690 - L'Annonciation de la Bienheureuse Vierge Marie (Oka) (Mission du Lac des Deux-Montagnes) (Mission St. Louis de Ile aux Tortes) L R T-Collaboration

PARISH: 1769 - St. Eustache (Riviere du Chene) L R *

PARISH: 1799 - St. Benoit (Mirabel) L R *

PARISH: 1825 - Ste Scholastique (Mirabel) L R *

PARISH: 1836 - St. Colomban R *

PARISH: 1837 - St. Hermas L R *

PARISH: 1838 - St. Augustin F-Maisonneuve

PARISH: 1850 - St. Placide L R *

PARISH: 1855 - St. Joseph du Lac L R *

PARISH: 1872 - Ste. Monique R *

PARISH: 1886 - St. Canut L R *

** T-Laliberte

* - Gauthier & Rivest (4 Volumes)

COUNTY: Dorchester *

LOCATION: South

REFERENCE: South of Quebec

MAP: 57

ARCHIVES: Quebec

CITY REFERENCE: Ste. Henedine

FIRST PARISH: 1824 - Ste. Claire

PARISH: 1829 - St. Edouard de Frampton

PARISH: 1830 - St. Anselme de Lauzon C-Goulet(deaths)

PARISH: 1834 - St. Isidore de Lauzon

PARISH: 1840 - Ste. Marguerite de Jolliet L Morissette

PARISH: 1844 - St. Bernard de Beauce

PARISH: 1852 - Ste. Henedine

PARISH: 1857 - St. Malachie de Frampton

PARISH: 1864 - Ste. Justine (Langevin) L

PARISH: 1867 - Ste. Germain du Lac Etchemin

PARISH; 1872 - St. Leon de Standon

PARISH: 1883 - St. Odilion de Cranbourne

PARISH: 1890 - St. Prosper

PARISH: 1893 - St. Maxime (Scott) C-Loveillo

PARISH: 1894 - Ste. Rose de Watford

* L-Frere Eloi-Gerard Talbot
  Q-Eloi-Gerard Talbot 11 Volumes (Beauce, Dorchester, Frontenac)

COUNTY: Drummond *

LOCATION: South

REFERENCE: South of Three Rivers

MAP: 45

ARCHIVES: Three Rivers

CITY REFERENCE: Drummondville **

FIRST PARISH: 1816 - St. Frederic de Drummondville J-Pontbriand
                        & Laliberte

PARISH: 1835 - St. Guillaume d'Upton L R J-Laliberte, Mongeau
                        & Pontbriand

PARISH: 1842 - St. Felix de Valois de Kingsey ** L

PARISH: 1850 - St. Pierre de Durham (L'Avenir) ** L

PARISH: 1859 - St. Germain de Grantham ** L

PARISH: 1864 - St. Fulgence de Durham (Durham Sud) ** L

PARISH: 1865 - St. Jean L'Evangeliste (Wickham) ** L

PARISH: 1866 - St. Bonaventure d'Upton L R J-Partenteau,
                        Laliberte & Pontbriand

PARISH: 1868 - Ste. Clothilde ** - see Arthabaska

PARISH: 1872 - St. Cyrille de Wendover ** L

PARISH: 1875 - St. Aime de Kingsey Falls **

PARISH: 1879 - St. Eugene de Grantham ** L R

PARISH: 1897 - Notre Dame de Bon Conseil ** L

PARISH: 1900 - St. Marjorique de Grantham **

PARISH: 1905 - St. Lucien **

* M-Thiverge (without St. Frederic)
* L-Fabien
** J-Provencher, Langlois & Jean (two volumes)
** J-Laliberte & Pontbriand (1850) (two volumes)

COUNTY: Frontenac   *

LOCATION: South

REFERENCE: Extreme south of Quebec, near Maine

MAP: 55

ARCHIVES: Sherbrooke

CITY REFERENCE: Lac Megantic

FIRST PARISH: 1848 - St. Vital de Lambton   - see Beauce

PARISH: 1855 - St. Evariste de Forsyth   - see Beauce

PARISH: 1857 - St. Gabriel de Stratford   - see Wolfe

PARISH: 1865 - St. Romain de Winslow   XX-Lambert

PARISH: 1868 - St. Pierre de Ditton   (La Patrie)   - see Compton

PARISH: 1869 - St. Sebastien   - see Beauce

PARISH: 1871 - St. Zenon   (Piopolis)

PARISH: 1872 - St. Samuel   L   (not in repertoire)

PARISH: 1877 - St. Ambroise (Notre Dame des Bois)

PARISH: 1887 - Ste. Cecile de Whitton   L

PARISH: 1889 - St. Methode de Frontenac   L

PARISH: 1892 - St. Leon   (Val Racine)

PARISH: 1896 - Ste. Agnes   (Lac Megantic)

PARISH: 1896 - St. Ludger

PARISH: 1898 - St. Augustin   (Woburn)

* M-Collaboration   (3 Volumes)
  F-Campagna
  L-Frere Eloi-Gerard Talbot
  Q-Eloi-Gerard Talbot   11 Volumes (Beauce, Dorchester, Frontenac)

COUNTY: Gaspe East *

LOCATION: Gaspe

REFERENCE: Eastern Tip of Gaspe

MAP: 69

ARCHIVES: Rimouski

CITY REFERENCE: Perce

FIRST PARISH: 1751 - Ste. Famille de Pabos **Arsenault

PARISH: 1800 - Ste. Claire de I'lle Perce

PARISH: 1801 - St. Michel de I'lle Perce **Arsenault

PARISH: 1845 - St. Patrick's de Douglastown (St. Patrice)

PARISH: 1851 - L'Assomption de Notre Dame de la Grande Riviere
               **Arsenault

PARISH: 1855 - St. Martin de la Riviere au Renard L XX-Ouellet

PARISH: 1864 - Ste. Adelaide de Pabos **Arsenault

PARISH: 1865 - St. Pierre de la Malbaie (Barachois)

PARISH: 1869 - St. Joseph de Cap d'Espoir **Arsenault

PARISH: 1869 - St. Albert de Gaspe

PARISH: 1869 - St. Dominique de Newport L **Arsenault

PARISH: 1871 - St. Georges de Malbaie

PARISH: 1872 - St. Alban du Cap des Rosiers XX-Ouellet

PARISH: 1873 - Ste. Cecile de Cloridorme L

PARISH: Grand Vallee L

** Chau T.V. - Television de la Baie des Chaleurs

* L-Gallant (1752-1850 Gaspesie)

COUNTY: Gaspe West *

LOCATION: Gaspe

REFERENCE: Extreme Southeast of Quebec

MAP: 68

ARCHIVES: Rimouski

CITY REFERENCE: Ste. Anne des Monts

FIRST PARISH: 1702 - Mont Louis

PARISH: 1824 - Ste. Anne des Monts

PARISH: 1864 - St. Norbert du Cap Chat

PARISH: 1867 - St. Maxime du Mont Louis

PARISH: 1874 - Ste. Marie Madeleine de Riviere Madeleine
                (Madeleine Center)

* GG - Denis-Riverin
* XX - Cahrbonneau

COUNTY: Gatineau *

LOCATION: North

REFERENCE: North of Ottawa

MAP: 18

ARCHIVES: Hull

CITY REFERENCE: Maniwaki

FIRST PARISH: 1840 - Notre Dame de L'Assomption de Maniwaki
(Mission de Warmontashing)
L   R   J-Provencher, Langlois & Jean

PARISH: 1841 - St. Paul d'Aylmer (Mission d'Aylmer) L   R
E-Collaboration, C-Beauregard, F-Perreault
J-Provencher, Langlois & Jean (Vol VI)

PARISH: 1841 - St. Joseph de Wakefield   F-Collaboration   K-
Provencher

PARISH: 1845 - St. Etienne de Chelsea - (St. Stephen)
(Old Chelsea)

PARISH: 1847 - St. Francois de Sales de Gatineau - see Hull

PARISH: 1850 - St. Camillus (Farrellton) R

PARISH: 1853 - Ste Cecile de la riviere a la Peche (Masham)
L   R   K-Provencher, F-Collaboration,

PARISH: 1856 - St. Columbkille (Pembroke) - in Ontario

PARISH: 1861 - Mission St. Cajetan

PARISH: 1861 - Ste. Famille d'Aumond L

PARISH: 1868 - Ste. Elizabeth de Cantley R   F-Collaboration,
E-Desormeaux

PARISH: 1868 - La Visitation de Notre Dame (Gracefield) L   R
F-Mennie de Varennes

PARISH: 1872 - St. Gabriel (Bouchette) R

PARISH: 1881 - Lac Ste Marie   K-Provencher & Jean

PARISH: 1883 - Perkins - see Papineau

PARISH: 1884 - St. Dominique d'Eardley (Luskville) R   K-Jean,
F-Bastien

52

PARISH: 1884 - Martindale

PARISH: 1891 - St. Pierre de Wakefield   R   E-Collaboration

PARISH: 1892 - Montcerf

* - TT. - Rivest

COUNTY: Hull

LOCATION: North

REFERENCE: North of Ottawa (From Gatineau & Papineau)

MAP: 19

ARCHIVES: Hull

CITY REFERENCE: Hull

FIRST PARISH: 1847 - St. Francois de Sales de Templeton (Pointe
                        Gatineau) R E-Roger, F-Houle,
                        J-(Vol VI)

PARISH: 1883 - Val des Monts (Perkins) - see Papineau

PARISH: 1886 - Notre Dame de Grace (Hull) E-McIntyre,
                Charbonneau & Dupuis J-(Vol III)

PARISH: 1890 - St. Rose de Lima - see Papineau

PARISH: 1902 - Tres St. Redempteur de Hull E-Collaboration

PARISH: 1913 - St. Joseph de Hull - (Wrightville)
                E-McIntyre, Charbonneau, Dupuis

J - L'Outaouais - Vol III- Provencher
    L'Outaouais - Vol VI - Provencher, Langlois & Jean

COUNTY: Huntingdon

LOCATION: Far South

REFERENCE: Near New York

MAP: 14

ARCHIVES: Montreal

CITY REFERENCE: Huntingdon

FIRST PARISH: 1764 - St. Jean Francois de St. Regis (Mission St. Regis) W-McDonald

PARISH: 1818 - St. Anicet - (Godmanchester) F-Campagna B-Campagna XX-Charette

PARISH: 1823 - St. Cyprien - see Napierville

PARISH: 1826 - St. Patrice de Hinchinbrooke (Herdman, Athelstan)

PARISH: 1849 - St. Romain de Hemmingford

PARISH: 1860 - St. Antoine Abbe (Franklin) L

PARISH: 1862 - St. Joseph de Huntingdon

PARISH: 1866 - Ste. Agnes de Dundee F-Campagna, B-Campagna XX-Chaette

PARISH: 1882 - Ste. Barbe L

COUNTY: Iberville *

LOCATION: South

REFERENCE: Southeast of Montreal

MAP: 8

ARCHIVES: Sherbrooke

CITY REFERENCE: Iberville

FIRST PARISH: 1823 - St. Athanase de Bleury L C-Bergeron,
                      F-Hamel, F-Lemieux

PARISH: 1828 - St. Jean d'Iberville - see St. Jean

PARISH: 1833 - St. Georges de Noyan (Henryville) L
                F-Lemieux

PARISH: 1841 - St. Gregoire la Grand (Mont St. Gregoire)
                L F-Lemieux

PARISH: 1842 - Christieville (Protestant)

PARISH: 1843 - Ste. Brigide L F-Lemieux

PARISH: 1843 - Trinity (Iberville) (Protestant)

PARISH: 1848 - Sabrevois (Protestant)

PARISH: 1851 - St. Alexandre L F-Lemieux

PARISH: 1851 - Caldwell & Christie Maners (Protestant)

PARISH: 1852 - Henryville (Protestant)

PARISH: 1864 - St. Sebastien F-Lemieux

PARISH: 1886 - Ste. Anne (Sabrevois) F-Collaboration

* L-Bergeron (Catholic & Protestant) 2 Volumes

COUNTY: I'le Montreal   (Hochlega & Jacques Cartier)

LOCATION: North

REFERENCE: Montreal

MAP: 72

ARCHIVES: Montreal

CITY REFERENCE: Montreal

FIRST PARISH: 1642 - Notre Dame de Montreal (Notre Dame de Nom de
             Marie) L C-Collaboration (post 1850)
             C-Bergeron,Brosseau, Gauthier (1642-1850)

PARISH: 1674 - L'Enfant Jesus Pointe aux Trembles (rural) L
         C-Collaboration

PARISH: 1676 - Sts. Anges de Lachine (rural) L C-Gareau &
         Bergeron

PARISH: 1685 - Mission de Montagne de Montreal

PARISH: 1687 - St. Joseph de la Riviere des Prairies (rural)
         L C-Bergeron

PARISH: 1687 - Ste.Anne de Bellevue (Boute de I'le) (rural)
         L C-Collaboration, F-Collaboration

PARISH: 1690 - Mission Aux Tortes   (Mission Lac des Deux
         Montagnes) - see Deux Montagnes

PARISH: 1711 - St. Joachim de Pointe Claire (rural) L
         C-Collaboration

PARISH: 1720 - St. Laurent (rural) L C-Gauthier & Legault

PARISH: 1724 - St. Francois d'Assise Longue Pointe (rural)
         C-Collaboration

PARISH: 1725 - Hospital General - la Misericorde (deaths) -
         XX-Raymond

PARISH: 1736 - La Visitation du Sault au Recollet (Notre Dame de
         Lorette, Fort Lorette) (rural) L R
         C-Bergeron, Brosseau & Gauthier

PARISH: 1741 - Ste. Genevieve de Pierrefonds (rural) L
         C-Collaboration

PARISH: 1755 - Hotel Dieu (deaths)

PARISH: 1844 - St. Raphael de I'le Bizard L C-Collaboration

PARISH: 1852 - Gesu (Montreal)

PARISH: 1856 - Notre Dame de Grace (montreal) L F-Hamelin

PARISH: 1859 - St. Patrice (Montreal) (English)

PARISH: 1862 - Marie Reine du Monde - see Montcalm

PARISH: 1862 - St. Jacques (Cathedrale) (Montreal)

PARISH: 1863 - St. Joseph (Hospice) (Montreal) C-Collaboration

PARISH: 1864 - St. Enfant Jesus du Mile End (Montreal)
                  F-Hamelin

PARISH: 1868 - La Nativite du la Bienheureuse Vierge Marie of
                  Hochlega (Montreal)

PARISH: 1868 - St. Henri des Tanneries - (Tanneries des
                  Rolland) (Montreal) F-Houle

PARISH: 1868 - St. Vincent de Paul (Montreal) F-Collaboration

PARISH: 1872 - St. Jacques le Majeur (Montreal) L-Collaboration

PARISH: 1873 - Ste. Brigide (Montreal) F-Hamelin

PARISH: 1873 - Ste. Anne (Montreal) (English)

PARISH: 1873 - St. Gabriel's Parish (Montreal) (English)

PARISH: 1873 - St. Joseph (Montreal) L-Collaboration

PARISH: 1873 - St. Jean de Dieu

PARISH: 1874 - Sacre Coeur de Jesus (Montreal) F-Charbonneau

PARISH: 1874 - St. Jean Bte. (Montreal)

PARISH: 1874 - St. Paul (Cote St. Paul) (Montreal)
                  C-Perodeau

PARISH: 1874 - Ste. Cunegonde (Montreal) C-Binette

PARISH: 1879 - Our Lady of Good Consel (English)

PARISH: 1882 - Pointe St. Charles F-Collaboration

PARISH: 1884 - St. Anthony (English)

PARISH: 1884 - Immaculee Conception

PARISH: 1884 - St. Benoit Joseph Labre

PARISH;   1886 - St. Leonard de Port Maurice C-LaChapelle

PARISH: 1888 - St. Louis de France   (Montreal)
                C-Collaboration, F-Collaboration

PARISH;   1888 - Tres St. Nom de Jesus   (Montreal)   F-Collaboration

PARISH: 1894 - Ste. Elizabeth du Portugal   (Montreal)
                F-Collaboration

PARISH: 1895 - St. Edouard de Montreal   C-Boulainne
                L-Collaboration

PARISH: 1895 - LaPresentation de la Sainte Vierge   (Dorval)
                C-Legault

PARISH: 1897 - St. Eusebe de Vercil   F-Fournier, Hamelin & Houle
                C-Collaboration

PARISH: 1898 - St. Pierre aux Liens   C-Legault

PARISH: 1898 - Notre Dame du St. Rosaire

PARISH: 1898 - St. Arsene

PARISH: 1899 - St. Denis

PARISH: 1899 - Notre Dame des Sept Douleurs de Verdun
                C-Monbleau

PARISH: 1899 - St. Clement de Viauville   F-Belanger

COUNTY: Iles de la Madeleine   * (Magdalen Islands)

LOCATION: Gaspe

REFERENCE: Off Prince Edward Island in Atlantic Ocean

MAP: none

ARCHIVES: Rimouski

CITY REFERENCE: Havre aux Maisons

FIRST PARISH: 1793 - Notre Dame de la Visitation   (Havre Aubert)

PARISH: 1824 - Ste. Madeleine   (Havre aux Maisons)

PARISH: 1850 - Holy Trinity   (Leslie - Grosse Ile) - Anglican

PARISH: 1873 - St. Francois Xavier   (Bassin)

PARISH: 1876 - St. Pierre   (Etang du Nord - La Vernier)

PARISH: 1886 - Sacre Coeur   (Grande Entree)

PARISH: All Saints   (Ile d'Entree) - Anglican

* Y-Boudreau

COUNTY: Joliette *

LOCATION: North

REFERENCE: East of Montreal

MAP: 25

ARCHIVES: Montreal

CITY REFERENCE: Joliette

FIRST PARISH: 1786 - St. Paul de Lavaltrie (Conversion de St. Paul) L R Q-Lepine-Amyot

PARISH: 1802 - Ste. Elizabeth (Dautray) L R Q-Collaboration

PARISH: 1832 - Ste. Melanie d'Ailleboust L R XX-Forest & Fortier

PARISH: 1832 - St. Ambroise de Kildare L R

PARISH: 1841 - St. Thomas L R XX-Leveille

PARISH: 1843 - St. Felix de Valois L R Q-Champagne

PARISH: 1843 - St. Charles Borromee de l'Industrie (Joliette Cathedrale) L R Q- Dufresne, Fortier & Gagnon Q-Riopel (BSM)

PARISH: 1844 - St. Alphonse de Rodriguez L R Q-Collaboration

PARISH: 1855 - St. Jean de Matha L R

PARISH: 1861 - Ste. Beatrix L R

PARISH: 1867 - St. Come L R XX-Leveille Q-Lepage

PARISH: 1870 - Ste. Emmelie de l'Energie L R

PARISH: 1871 - Mantawa

PARISH: 1897 - St. Cleophas L R

* TT.- Rivest

COUNTY: Kamouraska

LOCATION: South

REFERENCE: East of Quebec near Maine

MAP: 62

ARCHIVES: Quebec

CITY REFERENCE: St. Pascal

FIRST PARISH: 1685 - Notre Dame de Liesse (Riviere Quelle)
(Notre Dame de la Bouteillerie)
C-Collaboration P-Proulx

PARISH: 1715 - Ste. Anne de la Pocatiere (St. Anne de la Riviere
Sud) L C-Collaboration, K-Ouellet, P-Proulx

PARISH: 1727 - St. Louis de Kamouraska (Les Camourascas)
L P-Proulx

PARISH: 1791 - St. Andre de Kamouraska (Andreville) L
P-Proulx

PARISH: 1829 - St. Pascal L C-Collaboration P-Proulx

PARISH: 1841 - St. Denis de la Bouteillerie L
C-Collaboration P-Proulx

PARISH: 1850 - St. Alexandre de Kamouraska L P-Proulx

PARISH: 1850 - Ste. Helene de Kamouraska L P-Proulx

PARISH: 1853 - St. Pacome L C-Collaboration P-Proulx

PARISH: 1859 - Notre Dame du Mt. Carmel L C-Collaboration
P-Proulx

PARISH: 1864 - St. Onesime d'Ixworth P-Proulx XX-Ouellet

PARISH: 1870 - St. Philippe de Neri L C-Collaboration
P-Proulx

PARISH: 1874 - St. Eleuthere (Pohenegamook) L P-Proulx
XX-Theberge

PARISH: 1892 - St. Germain de Kamouraska R-Proulx

PARISH: 1893 - St. Bruno R-Proulx

COUNTY: LaBelle *

LOCATION: North

REFERENCE: North of Ottawa

MAP: 21

ARCHIVES: Hull/Montreal

CITY REFERENCE: Mont Laurier

FIRST PARISH: 1874 - Notre Dame du Laus L R

PARISH: 1882 - L'Annonciation R

PARISH: 1882 - La Conception R

PARISH: 1884 - Nomininque L R

PARISH: 1884 - Notre Dame de Pontmain R

PARISH: 1894 - Cathedrale Mont Laurier L R

PARISH: 1899 - St. Gerard - (Kiamika) R

PARISH: 1901 - Notre Dame du St. Sacrement - (Ferme Neuve) L

PARISH: 1901 - Lac des Ecorces

PARISH: 1901 - Ste. Veronique

* TT. - Rivest (3 Volumes)

COUNTY: Lac St. Jean Est (St. John's East) *

LOCATION: Far North

REFERENCE: Extreme North of Quebec

MAP: 33

ARCHIVES: Chicoutimi

CITY REFERENCE: Alma

FIRST PARISH: 1852 - Notre Dame d'Hebertville   L XX-Belanger

PARISH: 1869 - St. Jerome du Lac St. Jean   (Metabetchouan) L
                   XX-Belanger

PARISH: 1872 - St. Louis de Metabetchouan   (Chambord) O-Beaulieu

PARISH: 1872 - St. Prime -see Lac St. Jean Quest

PARISH: 1881 - St. Gedeon

PARISH: 1881 - St. Joseph d'Alma

PARISH: 1882 - St. Andre de Chambord   - see Lac St. Jean Quest
                   O-Beaulieu

PARISH: 1889 - St. Coeur de Marie

PARISH: 1891 - St. Bruno

PARISH: 1894 - Hebertville - Village

* P-Collaboration - with Societe Genealogique du Saguenay

COUNTY: Lac St. Jean Ouest   (St. John West) *
                               (Roberval)
LOCATION: Far North

REFERENCE: Extreme North of Quebec

MAP: 34

ARCHIVES: Chicoutimi

CITY REFERENCE: Roberval

FIRST PARISH: 1860 - Notre Dame du Lac (Roberval)   L O-Beaulieu
                      XX-Belanger

PARISH: 1861 - St. Jean Bte d L'Anse St. Jean

PARISH: 1872 - St. Prime O-Beaulieu XX-Belanger

PARISH: 1881 - St. Charles Borromee (Pointe Bleue)

PARISH: 1885 - St. Felicien

PARISH: 1888 - St. Methode O-Beaulieu

PARISH: 1890 - St. Thomas d'Aquin (Lac Bouchette) O-Beaulieu

PARISH: 1893 - Mistassini (James Bay) see - Abitibi

PARISH: 1895 - Normandin

PARISH: 1899 - St. Andre de Chambord O-Beaulieu

PARISH: 1903 - St. Francois de Sales O-Beaulieu

PARISH: 1907 - Ste. Hedwidge O-Beaulieu

PARISH: 1911 - Val Jalbert O-Beaulieu

* P-Collaboration with Societe Genealogique du Saguenay

COUNTY: LaPrairie *

LOCATION: South

REFERENCE: South of Montreal

MAP: 10

ARCHIVES: Montreal

CITY REFERENCE: LaPrairie

FIRST PARISH: 1670 - La Nativite de la Bienheureuse Vierge Marie
                (Notre Dame de la Prairie de la Madeleine)
                L   J-Jette

PARISH: 1724 - St. Francois Xavier de Sault St. Louis
                (Caughnawaga)

PARISH: 1752 - St. Constant (St. Pierre de la Tortue)   L

PARISH: 1753 - St. Philippe de LaPrairie (St. Jean Francois Regis
                in 1823)   L

PARISH: 1833 - St. Isidore L

PARISH: 1840 - St. Jacques le Mineur

PARISH: 1918 - St. Mathieu

*J-Jette (1751-1972)

COUNTY: L'Assomption *

LOCATION: North

REFERENCE: East of Montreal

MAP: 2

ARCHIVES: Montreal

CITY REFERENCE: L'Assomption

FIRST PARISH: 1679 - La Purification de la Bienheureuse Vierge
Marie de Repentigny L R
C-Rivest & Bergeron, F-Collaboration

PARISH: 1687 - St. Charles de Lachenaie L R

PARISH: 1706 - St. Sulpice L R L-Perreault

PARISH: 1724 - St. Pierre du Portage de L'Assomption L R
J-Pontbriand, F-Perreault (Deaths)

PARISH: 1750 - St. Henri Mascouche L

PARISH: 1787 - St. Roch de l'Achigan L R

PARISH: 1835 - St. Lin des Laurentides (Ville des Laurentides)
L R

PARISH: 1857 - L'Epiphanie L R L-Rivest

PARISH: 1857 - St. Paul L'Ermite (Le Gardeur) R

* TT.- Rivest

COUNTY: I'le Jesus (Laval)

LOCATION: North

REFERENCE: Northern Section of Montreal

MAP: 71

ARCHIVES: Montreal

CITY REFERENCE: Laval

FIRST PARISH: 1702 - St. Francois de Sales sur I'le Jesus
                    L R C-Bergeron L-Collaboration

PARISH: 1743 - St. Vincent de Paul   L R C-Bergeron & Gauthier

PARISH: 1745 - Ste. Rose de Lima de Laval L R C-Bergeron &
               Gauthier

PARISH: 1774 - St. Martin (Chomedey) L R C-Bergeron

PARISH: 1869 - Ste. Dorothee de Laval L C-Bergeron & Gauthier

PARISH: 1895 - Soeurs du Bon Pasteur (Laval des Rapides)
               (Pont Viau)

PARISH: 1900 - St. Elzear de Laval (Cap St. Martin)
                    R C-Bergeron & Gauthier

PARISH: 1915 - St. Christophe (Pont Viau) R L-Collaboration

COUNTY: Levis

LOCATION: South

REFERENCE: South of Quebec

MAP: 56

ARCHIVES: Quebec

CITY REFERENCE: St. Romuald

FIRST PARISH: 1679 - St. Joseph de la Pointe Levy (Lauzon)
                   L   J-Talbot & St. Hilaire

PARISH: 1694 - St. Nicholas L J-Pontbriand & Gingras
              Z- Oliver (BM), Gingras (deaths)

PARISH: 1766 - St. Henri de Lauzon L C-Goulet (deaths), J-Talbot

PARISH: 1830 - St. Jean Chrysostome (Lauzon) L
              J- St. Hilaire, Talbot & Pontbriand

PARISH: 1851 - Notre Dame de la Victoire de Levis L
              J-Pontbriand

PARISH: 1854 - St. Lambert de Lauzon L   J-Talbot &
              Pontbriand

PARISH: 1854 - St. Romuald d'Etchemin L
              J-St. Hilaire, Talbot & Pontbriand

PARISH: 1861 - St. Etienne de Lauzon L
              J-Talbot & Pontbriand

PARISH: 1877 - St. David de l'Aube Riviere L
              J- Talbot & Pontbriand

PARISH: 1896 - St. Antoine de Blenville J-Pontbriand

PARISH: 1899 - St. Louis de Pintendre J-Talbot

COUNTY: L'Islet *

LOCATION: South

REFERENCE: East of Quebec near Maine

MAP: 61

ARCHIVES: Quebec

CITY REFERENCE: St. Jean Port Joli

FIRST PARISH: 1679 - Notre Dame de Bonsecours de L'Islet sur Mer
L C-Collaboration R-Proulx

PARISH: 1734 - St.Roch des Aulnaies L C-Collaboration
P-Proulx

PARISH: 1767 - St. Jean (Port Joli) L C-Proulx

PARISH: 1858 - St. Aubert L R-Proulx

PARISH: 1859 - Ste. Louise des Aulnaies P-Proulx

PARISH: 1865 - St. Cyrille de Lessard L C-Proulx

PARISH: 1869 - Ste. Perpetue R-Proulx

PARISH: 1874 - St. Eugene L C-Collaboration R-Proulx

PARISH: 1880 - St. Pamphile R-Proulx

PARISH: 1889 - St. Damase des Aulnaies P-Proulx

PARISH: 1890 - St. Adalbert R-Proulx

PARISH: 1894 - St. Marcel R-Proulx

* Q- Eloi-Gerard Talbot 16 Volumes (Montmagny, L'Islet,
Bellechasse)

COUNTY: Lotbiniere *

LOCATION: South

REFERENCE: Southwest of Quebec

MAP: 53

ARCHIVES: Quebec

CITY REFERENCE: Ste. Croix

FIRST PARISH: 1697 - St. Louis de Lotbiniere L J-Collaboration
               J-Talbot & Pontbriand

PARISH: 1702 - St. Antoine de Tilly (St. Antoine de Pade)
               L J-Pontbriand

PARISH: 1714 - Ste. Croix de Lotbiniere L J-Collaboration

PARISH: 1741 - St. Jean Bte Deschaillons L J-Pontbriand

PARISH: 1829 - St. Gilles de Beaurivage L J-Pontbriand & Gingras

PARISH: 1829 - St. Sylvestre L J-Pontbriand & Gingras

PARISH: 1857 - Ste. Agathe L J-Pontbriand & Gingras

PARISH: 1856 - St. Flavien L J-Talbot** & Pontbriand
               XX-LeMay

PARISH; 1856 - St. Apollinaire L J-Talbot & Pontbriand

PARISH: 1863 - St. Edouard de Lotbiniere L
               J-Hebert, Talbot & Pontbriand

PARISH: 1864 - Ste. Emmelie (Leclercville) L
               J-Hebert, Talbot & Pontbriand

PARISH: 1867 - St. Agapit de Beaurivage L J-Talbot & Pontbriand

PARISH: 1871 - St. Patrice de Beaurivage L J-Pontbriand &
               Gingras

PARISH: 1873 - St. Narcisse de Beaurivage L J-Pontbriand &
               Gingras

PARISH: 1881 - Ste. Philomene de Fortierville L J-Pontbriand

PARISH: 1900 - St. Jacques (Parisville) L J-Pontbriand

PARISH: 1903 - Notre Dame (Issoudun) - J-Hebert, Talbot &
               Pontbriand

PARISH: 1912 - St. Octave (Dosquet) L J-Talbot & Pontbriand

* J-Collaboration (1838-1967)
  J- St. Hilaire
** Talbot = Brother Eloi-Gerard Talbot

COUNTY: Maskinonge

LOCATION: North

REFERENCE: West of Three Rivers

MAP: 27

ARCHIVES: Three Rivers

CITY REFERENCE: Louiseville

FIRST PARISH: 1714 - St. Antoine de la Riviere du Loup
                      (Louiseville) L F-Campagna

PARISH: 1728 - St. Joseph de Maskinonge L F-Campagna

PARISH: 1770 - St. Cuthbert   - see Berthier

PARISH: 1802 - St. Leon le Grand L F-Campagna

PARISH: 1842 - St. Alexis de la Grande Baie (Ville de la Baie)
                see Chicoutimi

PARISH: 1842 - Ste. Ursule XX-Legare

PARISH: 1850 - St. Paulin C-Collaboration

PARISH: 1853 - St. Didace L

PARISH: 1858 - St. Justin L C-Collaboration XX-Plante

PARISH: 1872 - St. Alexis des Monts C-Doucet, P-LeMay -Doucet

PARISH: 1905 - St. Ignance du Lac C - Rivest & LaSalle

PARISH: 1915 - St. Edouard O-Collaboration

PARISH: 1917 - Ste. Angele de Premont O-Collaboration

COUNTY: Matane *

LOCATION: Gaspe

REFERENCE: Northwest Gaspe, Southeast of Baie Comeau

MAP: 67

ARCHIVES: Rimouski

CITY REFERENCE: Matane

FIRST PARISH: 1812 - St. Jerome de Matane S-Volume 1

PARISH: 1855 - St. Octave de Metis P-Volume 5

PARISH: 1860 - L'Assomption de Notre Dame (Baie des Sables)
                  (Mc Nider) P-Volume 2

PARISH: 1864 - Ste. Felicite - S-Volume 2

PARISH: 1868 - St. Ulric de Riviere Blanche P-Volume 2

PARISH: 1880 - Mission de St. Edouard les Mechins S-Volume 2

PARISH: 1889 - Sts. Sept Freres (Grosses-Roches) S-Volume 2

PARISH: 1891 - St. Luc S-Volume 2   P-Volume 5

* S- Comeau, Roy & Beaulieu Volume 1 - 1819-1988 - Matane
                              Volume 2 - 1865-1988 - Est de Matane

* P- Collaboration with Societe Genealogique de l'Est du Quebec
     5 Volumes (Volume 2 - Quest de Matane, Volume 5 - La Mitis
          Mont Joli)

* XX-Charbonneau

COUNTY: Matapedia *

LOCATION: Gaspe

REFERENCE: Northwestern Gaspe near New Brunswick

MAP: 66

ARCHIVES: Rimouski

CITY REFERENCE: Amqui

FIRST PARISH: 1870 - St. Benoit-Joseph-Labre (Amqui)
                        C-Goulet P-Vol 3
PARISH: 1871 - St. Alexis de Matapedia - see Bonaventure

PARISH: 1873 - St. Moise C-Goulet P-Vol 3

PARISH: 1879 - Missions d l'Intercolonial

PARISH: 1883 - St. Damase C-Goulet P-Vol2

PARISH: 1884 - St. Pierre du Lac (Val Brillant)
                     C-Goulet P-Vol3

PARISH: 1884 - St. Jacques (Causapscal) C-Goulet P-Vol3

PARISH: 1895 - St. Nom de Marie (Sayabec) C-Goulet P-Vol3

PARISH: 1905 - St. Leon le Grand C-Goulet P-Vol3

PARISH: 1907 - St. Edmond (Lac au Saumon) C-Goulet P-Vol 3

PARISH: 1909 - Ste. Florence C-Goulet P-Vol3

PARISH: 1910 - St. Antoine (Padoue) C-Goulet P-Vol2

PARISH: 1918 - St. Zenon (Lac Humqui) C-Goulet P-Vol3

PARISH: 1919 - St. Raphael (Albertville) C-Goulet P-Vol3

* P-Collaboration with Societe Genealogique de l'Est du Quebec
  5 Volumes (Volume 3 Vallee de la Matapedia)

* XX-Charbonneau

COUNTY: Megantic *

LOCATION: South

REFERENCE: Southwest of Quebec

MAP: 54

ARCHIVES: Quebec

CITY REFERENCE: Inverness

FIRST PARISH: 1840 - St. Calixte de Somerset (Plessisville) L

PARISH: 1847 - St. Ferdinand d'Halifax (Bernierville) L

PARISH: 1854 - Ste. Julie de Somerset (Laurierville) L

PARISH: 1855 - Ste. Sophie d'Halifax (Halifax-Nord) L
            XX-Lapointe

PARISH: 1855 - St. Jacques (Leeds) NN-Collaboration
            XX-Laflamme

PARISH: 1855 - St. Pierre de Broughton - see Beauce

PARISH: 1859 - St. Athanase d'Inverness L

PARISH: 1869 - Ste. Anastasie de Nelson (Lyster) L

PARISH: 1879 - Sacre Coeur de Marie (Thetford Mission)
            NN-Collaboration

PARISH: 1879 - St. Adrien d'Irlande L

PARISH: 1886 - St. Pierre de Baptiste

PARISH: 1886 - St. Alphonse Thetford Mines

PARISH: 1890 - St. Desire du Lac Noir (Black Lake) L

PARISH: 1893 - Notre Dame de Lourdes L

PARISH: 1898 - St. Antoine de Pontbriand

* M-Collaboration (2 Volumes)
* F-Campagna
* L-Fabien

COUNTY: Missisquoi *

LOCATION: Far South

REFERENCE: Southeast of Montreal near Vermont

MAP: 40

ARCHIVES: Sherbrooke

CITY REFERENCE: Bedford

FIRST PARISH: 1846 - Notre Dame des Anges (Stanbridge)

PARISH: 1850 - Ste. Croix (Dunham)

PARISH: 1850 - St. Romuald (Farnham) L Q-Boisvenue

PARISH: 1869 - St. Damien Bedford L

PARISH: 1874 - Notre Dame de Lourdes (St. Armand Quest)

PARISH: 1876 - Ste. Rose de Lima (Cowansville) (in Brome
                 repertoire)

PARISH: 1877 - St. Ignance (Stanbridge) L

PARISH: 1877 - Ste. Rose de Lima (Sweetsburg)

PARISH: 1885 - St. Jacques le Majeur (Clarenceville) L

PARISH: 1886 - St. Francois de Assise (Frelighsburg) L

PARISH: 1888 - Ste. Sabine

PARISH: 1892 - St. Pierre de Verone (Pike River)

PARISH: 1925 - St. Philippe (Philipsburg)

PARISH: 1928 - Ste. Therese (Cowansville)

* J-Pontbriand & Jette

COUNTY: Montcalm *

LOCATION: North

REFERENCE: Northeast of Montreal

MAP: 24

ARCHIVES: Montreal

CITY REFERENCE: Ste. Julienne

FIRST PARISH: 1774 - St. Jacques de l'Achigan   L   R   Q-Leblanc

PARISH: 1808 - St. Esprit (St. Ours)   L   R   Q-Leblanc

PARISH: 1837 - St. Patrice de Rawdon   (Marie Reine du Monde)
                 L   R   Q-Collaboration

PARISH: 1849 - Ste. Julienne de Montcalm   L   R   Q-Rivest
                 QQ-Collaboration

PARISH: 1849 - St. Alexis   L   R   Q-Leblanc

PARISH: 1852 - St. Ligouri   L   R   Q-Leveille & Amyot

PARISH: 1854 - St. Calixte   L   R

PARISH: 1858 - St. Theodore de Chertsey   L   R   XX-Collaboration

PARISH: 1873 - St. Donat

PARISH: 1888 - Ste Marie Solomee   R   Q-Melancon

PARISH: 1891 - Notre Dame de la Merci   L   R

PARISH: 1898 - St. Emile   R   Q-Webster & Chevalier

* TT.- Rivest

COUNTY: Montmagny *

LOCATION: South

REFERENCE: East of Quebec

MAP: 60

ARCHIVES: Quebec

CITY REFERENCE: Montmagny

FIRST PARISH: 1679 - St. Thomas de la Pointe a la Caille
(Montmagny) L R-Proulx

PARISH: 1682 - St. Ignance du Cap St. Ignance L C-Collaboration
R-Proulx

PARISH: 1710 - Notre Dame de l'Assomption de Bellechasse
(Berthier) (Berthier Sur Mer) C-Collaboration
R-Proulx

PARISH: 1727 - St. Pierre de la Riviere du Sud C-Collaboration

PARISH: 1734 - St. Francois de la Riviere du Sud C-Collaboration
R-Proulx

PARISH: 1831 - St. Antoine de I'lle Aux Grues L C-Collaboration
R-Proulx

PARISH: 1834 - St. Luc (Grosse I'le) L C-Collaboration R-
Proulx

PARISH: 1868 - St. Paul de Buton (Montminy) L R-Proulx
C-Goulet (deaths)

PARISH: 1889 - Notre Dame du Rosarie C-Goulet (deaths) R-Proulx

PARISH: 1902 - Ste. Appolline R-Proulx

PARISH: 1904 - St. Fabien de Panet

PARISH: 1907 - St. Euphemie C-Goulet (deaths)

* Q- Eloi-Gerard Talbot - 16 Volumes (Montmagny, L'Islet,
Bellechasse

COUNTY: Montmorency #1

LOCATION: North

REFERENCE: East of Quebec

MAP: 32

ARCHIVES: Quebec

CITY REFERENCE: Chateau Richer

FIRST PARISH: 1657 - Ste. Anne de Beaupre (St. Anne du Petit
                    Cap) L K-Edmond, P-Gingras

PARISH: 1661 - Notre Dame de la Visitation (Chateau Richer)
                 L P-St. Pierre

PARISH: 1670 - L'Ange Gardien L J-Pontbriand

PARISH: 1687 - St. Joachim L K-Edmond P-Gingras

PARISH: 1806 - St. Ferreol les Neiges L P-Gingras

PARISH: 1835 - Ste. Brigitte de Laval L J-Ross, Gingras &
                 Pontbriand

PARISH: 1867 - St. Tite des Caps L P-Gingras

PARISH: 1891 - St. Gregoire de Montmorency L P-Gingras

COUNTY: Montmorency #2 (I'le de Orleans) *

LOCATION: North

REFERENCE: Quebec/St. Lawrence River

MAP: 74

ARCHIVES: Quebec

CITY REFERENCE: Ste. Famille

FIRST PARISH: 1666 - Ste. Famille L K-Bureau, Dumas & Tessier

PARISH: 1679 - St. Pierre & St. Paul L

PARISH: 1679 - St. Laurent L

PARISH: 1679 - St. Francois de Sales L

PARISH: 1680 - St. Jean Baptiste L

PARISH: 1872 - Ste. Petronille de Beaulieu L

* K-Bureau, Dumas & Tessier
  P-Bureau, Dumas, Tessier & Turgeon (2 Volumes)

COUNTY: Napierville *

LOCATION: South

REFERENCE: South of Montreal

MAP: 13

ARCHIVES: Montreal

CITY REFERENCE: Napierville

FIRST PARISH: 1823 - St. Cyprien de Lery (Napierville) L

PARISH: 1830 - St. Remi de La Salle

PARISH: 1833 - St. Edouard de Napierville

PARISH: 1849 - St. Romain de Hemmingford - see Huntingdon

PARISH: 1853 - St. Patrice de Sherrington

PARISH: 1854 - St. Michel Archange L XX-Fabien

* J-Pontbriand

COUNTY: Nicolet *

LOCATION: South

REFERENCE: South of Three Rivers

MAP: 49

ARCHIVES: Three Rivers

CITY REFERENCE: Becancour

FIRST PARISH: 1716 - La Nativite de Notre Dame & St. Pierre de
                     Becancour L F-Campagna

PARISH: 1716 - St. Jean Baptiste de Nicolet L F-Allard

PARISH: 1734 - St. Pierre les Becquets L F-Campagna

PARISH: 1784 - St. Edouard de Gentilly L F-Campagna

PARISH: 1802 - St. Gregoire le Grand L F-Allard & Labonte

PARISH: 1844 - Ste. Monique L F-Campagna, B-Morin & Allard,
                     O-Lemire (B&S)

PARISH: 1849 - Ste. Gertrude (Becancour) L F-Campagna

PARISH: 1851 - St. Celestin (Almaville) L F-Bergeron

PARISH: 1862 - Ste. Brigitte des Saults L O-Gelinas

PARISH: 1866 - St. Leonard d'Aston

PARISH: 1868 - St. Wenceslas

PARISH: 1870 - Ste. Angele de Laval F-Campagna

PARISH: 1872 - Ste. Marie de Blandford

PARISH: 1874 - Ste. Perpetue L

PARISH: 1874 - Ste. Sophie de Levrard

PARISH: 1876 - Ste. Eulalie L

PARISH: 1888 - St. Sylvere XX-Dubois

PARISH: 1890 - St. Samuel

* M-Collaboration (4 Volumes)
* XX-Abbott-Corriveau

COUNTY:Ottawa *

LOCATION: Ontario

REFERENCE: around Ottawa

MAP: not referenced

ARCHIVES: Ottawa

CITY REFERENCE: Ottawa

FIRST PARISH: 1829 - Notre Dame de Ottawa (La Cathedrale)   L
                      J-Provencher & Langlois (Vol IV)
                      F-Collaboration

PARISH: 1836 - L'Original   L   J-Provencher (VolV)

PARISH: 1839 - Curran J-Provencher (VolV)

PARISH: 1849 - La Visitation de Ottawa

PARISH: 1853 - Ste. Angelique - see Papineau

PARISH: 1855 - Clarence Creek   L   J-Provencher (Vol V)

PARISH: 1856 - St. Joseph Ottawa   F-Dufor,Dumouchel, Hamelin

PARISH: 1857 - St. Malachie

PARISH: 1859 - Orleans   J-Provencher (VolV)

PARISH: 1864 - L'Ange Gardien d'Angers   E-Delisle   J-Provencher
                      & Jean (VolI & II)

PARISH: 1868 - Notre Dame de Bonsecours

PARISH: 1873 - Ste Anne Ottawa   J-Provencher & Langlois
                      (Vol IV) F-Joly

PARISH: 1873 - Notre Dame de Lourdes de Cyrville   U-Lavergne

PARISH: 1882 - St. Joachim   U-Brule & Chiasson

PARISH: 1887 - Rockland J-Provencher (VOL V)

PARISH: 1889 - Notre Dame de Bon Conseil   J-Provencher & Langlois
                      (Vol IV)

PARISH: 1889 - Ste. Brigide   F-Hamelin

PARISH: 1889 - Sacre Coeur   F-Hamelin

PARISH: 1891 - St. Francois D'Assise D'Ottawa   K-Langlois

* F-Collaboration

85

COUNTY: Papineau

LOCATION: North

REFERENCE: North of Ottawa

MAP: 20

ARCHIVES: Hull

CITY REFERENCE: Papineauville

FIRST PARISH: 1815 - Notre Dame de Bonsecours del la Petite Nation
(Montebello) (Bouchette)
F-Collaboration, E-Collaboration,
J-Provencher & Jean (Vol I & II)

PARISH: 1836 - St. Gregorie de Nazianze Mission de Buckingham L
E-Therriault, J-Provencher, Langlois & Jean
(Vol VI), F-Therriault

PARISH: 1851 - St. Andre Avellin L J-Provencher & Jean (I & II)

PARISH: 1853 - Ste. Angelique (Papineauville) E-Collaboration,
J-Provencher & Jean (Vol I & II)

PARISH: 1864 - L'Ange Gardien (Angers) - see Ottawa

PARISH: 1864 - St. Jean Evangeliste (Thurso) · E-Chenier & Roger
J-Provencher & Jean (Vol I & II)

PARISH: 1866 - St. Casmir de Ripon K-Provencher, Seguin & Jean
E-Seguin - Therriault

PARISH: 1874 - St. Felix de Valois (Cheneville) E-Therriault
J-Provencher, Langlois & Jean (Vol VI)

PARISH: 1882 - Ste. Valerie - (Boileau)

PARISH: 1883 - Val des Monts (St. Antoine de Perkins)
J-Provencher & Jean (I & II)

PARISH: 1883 - Notre Dame de la Salette L K-Provencher & Jean

PARISH: 1886 - St. Malachie E-Chenier & Roger

PARISH: 1886 - Notre Dame de Luminiers de Mayo E-Chenier & Roger

PARISH: 1887 - Masson L J-Provencher & Jean (I & II)

PARISH: 1888 - Notre Dame du Mont Carmel (Duhamel) J-Provencher,
Roger & Jean (Vol VI)

PARISH: 1890 - Ste. Rose de Lima L K-Jean - moved to Hull

PARISH: 1891 - St. Sixte F-Seguin J-Provencher & Jean (I&II)

PARISH: 1891 - Notre Dame de la Garde (Val des Bois) E-Desormeaux
                  J-Provencher & Jean (Vol I&II)

PARISH: 1891 - St. Louis de Poltimore E-Desormeaux K-Provencher
                  & Jean

PARISH: 1899 - St. Emile de Suffolk E-Chenier & Roger
                  J-Provencher, Langlois & Jean (Vol VI)

PARISH: 1901 - Coeur Tres Pur de Marie - (Plaisance)
                  E-Collaboration J-Provencher, Langlois
                  & Jean (VolVI)
PARISH: 1902 - Notre Dame de la Paix - J-Provencher, Langlois &
                  Jean (Vol VI)

PARISH: 1902 - Notre Dame de la Conception - (Montpellier)

J- L'Outaouais - Volumes I-VI

COUNTY: Pontiac *

LOCATION: North

REFERENCE: Northwest of Ottawa

MAP: 17

ARCHIVES: Hull

CITY REFERENCE: Campbell's Bay

FIRST PARISH: 1823 - St. Paul's Shawville   F-Collaboration
(Anglican)

PARISH: 1845 - St. Etienne de Chelsea (St. Stephen) - see
Gatineau

PARISH: 1846 - St. Alphonsus de Iles des Allumettes (Chapeau)

PARISH: 1846 - Ste. Anne   (Ile du Grand Calumet)

PARISH: 1847 - Ste. Brigid's of North Onslow

PARISH: 1848 - Ste. Mary Quyon (North Onslow)

PARISH: 1851 - St. Jacques le Majeur (St. James) (Portage du Fort)
F-Collaboration

PARISH: 1851 - Our Lady of Mt. Carmel (LaPasse) - Ontario

PARISH: 1851 - St. Alexandre Charteris (Clarendon)
F-Collaboration

PARISH: 1856 - St. Columbkille (Pembroke) - Ontario

PARISH: 1857 - St. John Evangeliste (Quyon) (Anglican)

PARISH: 1863 - St. Paul the Hermit (Sheenboro)
(Mission de Fort William)

PARISH: 1871 - Otter Lake (Leslie)

PARISH: 1875 - Ste. Elizabeth (Vinton)

PARISH: 1884 - St. Pierre (Fort Coulonge)

PARISH: 1884 - St. Dominique (Luskville) - see Gatineau

PARISH: 1895 - Ste. Sophie (East Aldfield) (Wolf Lake)

PARISH: 1895 - St. Francis Xavier

*C-Ouimet & Collaboration

COUNTY: Portneuf *

LOCATION: North

REFERENCE: West of Quebec

MAP: 30

ARCHIVES: Quebec

CITY REFERENCE: Cap Sante

FIRST PARISH: 1679 - Ste. Famille du Cap Sante L

PARISH: 1679 - St. Francois de Sales de Neuville
                (Pt. Aux Trembles) L J-Pontbriand

PARISH: 1680 - St. Charles des Roches des Grondines
                L J-Pontbriand

PARISH: 1693 - St. Augustin de Desmaures L

PARISH: 1705 - St. Joseph de Deschambault L

PARISH: 1742 - St. Jean Bte des Ecureuils (Donnacona)
                L J-Jette

PARISH: 1832 - Ste. Catherine de Fossambault L J-Pontbriand

PARISH: 1844 - St. Raymond (Nonnat) L J-Pontbriand

PARISH: 1847 - St. Basile L J-Pontbriand

PARISH: 1847 - St. Casimir L K-Tessier

PARISH: 1856 - St. Alban de Deschambault L

PARISH: 1861 - Notre Dame des Sept Douleurs (Portneuf)
                L

PARISH: 1869 - Ste. Jeanne de Neuville (Pont Rouge)
                L

PARISH: 1871 - St. Ubald L

PARISH: 1881 - Notre Dame des Anges des Montauban

PARISH: 1890 - St. Bernardin (Riviere a Pierre)

PARISH: 1893 - St. Gilbert de Deschambault L

PARISH: 1895 - Ste. Christine

PARISH: 1897 - St. Remi (Lac au Sable)

PARISH: 1898 St. Thuribe

PARISH: 1899 - St. Leonard   L

* J-Pontbriand   2 Volumes   (1679 - 1900, 1881 - 1950)

COUNTY: Quebec

LOCATION: North

REFERENCE: at Quebec

MAP: 31

ARCHIVES: Quebec

CITY REFERENCE: Quebec

FIRST PARISH: 1621 - Notre Dame de l'Immaculee Conception
                       L   J-Pontbriand

PARISH: 1638 - Mission St. Joseph - Sillery J-1

PARISH: 1665 - Hotel Dieu Quebec (deaths)

PARISH: 1673 - La Nativite de Notre Dame de Beauport (Notre
                Dame de la Misericorde) L J-Pontbriand
                P-Gingras XX-Giroux

PARISH: 1676 - Notre Dame de l'Annonciation de l'Ancienne Lorette
                L K-Provencher, P-Provencher L-Pagcot

PARISH: 1679 - St. Charles Borromee de Charlesbourg
                L J-Pontbriand

PARISH: 1679 - Ste. Foy - (Notre Dame de Foy) L J-Pontbriand &
                Gingras

PARISH: 1728 - Notre Dames des Anges (L'Hopital General
                Quebec) K-Pontbriand

PARISH: 1761 - St. Ambroise de la Jeune Lorette (Loretteville)
                (Mission des Hurons) (Notre Dame de la Jeune -
                Lorette) L J-Provencher

PARISH: 1829 - St. Roch de Quebec L J-Pontbriand (3 Vol)

PARISH: 1834 - St. Dunstan du Lac Beauport
                J- Ross, Gingras & Pontbriand

PARISH: 1834 - Ste. Brigitte de Laval - see Montmorency #1

PARISH: 1843 - St. Gabriel Valcartier L J-Ross, Gingras &
                Pontbriand

PARISH: 1847 - Hopital de la Marine

PARISH: 1851 - St. Edmond de Stoneham L J-Ross, Gingras &
                Pontbriand

PARISH: 1855 - St. Michel Archange (asile) C-Gaboury (1896)

PARISH: 1855 - St. Colomb de Sillery J-Pontbriand & Gingras

PARISH: 1856 - St. Patrick de Quebec

PARISH: 1860 - St. Michel's Chapel - Sillery (Anglican)
                J-Pontbriand

PARISH: 1860 - St. Jean Baptiste L P-Doddridge

PARISH: 1862 - St. Felix de Cap Rouge L J-Pontbriand

PARISH: 1867 - St. Sauveur de Quebec L P-Roberge

PARISH: 1874 - Notre Dame du Sacre Coeur J-Gaboury

PARISH: 1877 - Notre Dame de la Garde XX-Ross

PARISH: 1891 - Villeneuve

PARISH: 1896 - St. Zephirin de Stadacona L C-Gaboury

PARISH: 1896 - St. Charles de Limoilou P-Roberge

PARISH: 1899 - St. Malo P-St. Pierre

PARISH: 1901 - Notre Dame de Jacques Cartier J-Gaboury

PARISH: 1904 - Notre Dame de Lorette (Village des Hurons)
                J-Pontbriand

COUNTY: Richelieu

LOCATION: South

REFERENCE: West of Three Rivers

MAP: 3

ARCHIVES: Sherbrooke/Montreal

CITY REFERENCE: Sorel **

FIRST PARISH: 1670 - St. Pierre de Sorel L R J-Mongeau (2
                      Volumes 1675-1966) Q-Collaboration

PARISH: 1727 - L'Immaculee Conception de St. Ours L R
                J-Cournoyer C-Collaboration

PARISH: 1757 - Fort St. Jean - see St. Jean

PARISH: 1784 - Christ Church de Sorel (Protestant) R **

PARISH: 1836 - St. Aime (Massueville) L R J-Laliberte

PARISH: 1843 - Ste. Victoire L R **

PARISH: 1855 - St. Marcel L R J-Laliberte & Mongeau

PARISH: 1855 - St. Robert L R J-Laliberte & Mongeau
                XX-Cournoyer

PARISH: 1859 - St. Roch de Richelieu L' R J- I.Jette
                XX-Cournoyer

PARISH: 1875 - St. Joseph de Sorel R **

PARISH: 1876 - Ste. Anne de Sorel L R **

PARISH: 1876 - St. Louis de Bonsecours L R J-Laliberte & Jette

PARISH: 1911 - Notre Dame de Perpetule Secours R **

* XX-Dejorday - genealogy 2 Volumes (1784-1973)
** J-Mongeau & Laliberte

COUNTY: Richmond *

LOCATION: South

REFERENCE: Extreme South of Three Rivers

MAP: 46

ARCHIVES:

CITY REFERENCE: Richmond

FIRST PARISH: 1847 - Mission du Canton de Shipton

PARISH: 1851 - Ste. Bibiane de Cleveland de Richmond L

PARISH: 1864 - St. Georges de Windsor

PARISH: 1866 - Ste. Anne de Danville

PARISH: 1872 - Ste. Praxede de Brompton Falls (Bromptonville) L

PARISH: 1873 - St. Philippe de Windsor Mills

PARISH: 1875 - St. Philemon de Stoke (Stoke Centre) L

PARISH: 1885 - St. Francis Xavier de Brompton

PARISH: 1897 - St. Aime (Asbestos)

PARISH: 1900 - St. Claude

* M-Collaboration (3 Volumes)
* F-Campagna

COUNTY: Rimouski *

LOCATION: Gaspe

REFERENCE: Northwestern Gaspe near New Brunswick

MAP: 65

ARCHIVES: Rimouski

CITY REFERENCE: Rimouski

FIRST PARISH: 1699 - St. Germain de Rimouski   C-Goulet   P-Vol4

PARISH: 1836 - St. Simon   C-Goulet   P-Vol1

PARISH: 1842 - Ste. Luce   C-Goulet   P-Vol5

PARISH: 1848 - St. Fabien   C-Goulet   P-Vol1   XX-Riou

PARISH: 1850 - Ste. Cecile du Bic   C-Goulet   P-Vol1   XX-Chenard

PARISH: 1850 - Ste. Flavie   C-Goulet   P-Vol5

PARISH: 1855 - St. Octave de Metis - see Matane

PARISH: 1859 - St. Anclet de Lessard   C-Goulet   P-Vol4

PARISH: 1864 - Ste. Felicite - see Matane

PARISH: 1866 - St. Mathieu de Rioux   C-Goulet P-Vol1
                C-Chenard

PARISH: 1868 - Ste. Angele de Merci   C-Goulet   P-Vol5

PARISH: 1869 - St. Donat   P-Vol5

PARISH: 1873 - St. Gabriel   C-Goulet   P-Vol5

PARISH: 1874 - St. Joseph de Lepage (Mont Joli)   C-Goulet P-Vol5

PARISH: 1875 - Notre Dame du Sacre Coeur   C-Goulet   P-Vol4

PARISH: 1881 - Ste. Blandine   C-Goulet   P-Vol4

PARISH: 1882 - Ste. Anne de la Pointe au Pere   C-Goulet   P-Vol4

PARISH: 1885 - St. Valerien   C-Goulet   P-Vol1   C-Chenard

PARISH: 1889 - Notre Dame de Lourdes   P-Vol5

* P-Collaboration with Societe Genealogique de l'Est du Quebec
  5 Volumes (Matane. Matapedia, Rimouski, Mt. Joli)

Volume 1 - Quest de Rimouski
Volume 4 -Rimouski
Volume 5 -La Mitis Mt. Joli

COUNTY: Riviere du Loup   *

LOCATION: South

REFERENCE: Extreme east, start of Gaspe

MAP: 63

ARCHIVES: Quebec

CITY REFERENCE: Riviere du Loup

FIRST PARISH: 1713 - Notre Dame des Neiges   (Trois Pistoles)
                        C-Collaboration, P- Volume 3   XX-Lemay

PARISH: 1766 - St. Jean Bte (I'lle Verte)   P-Volume 2   XX-lemay

PARISH: 1813 - St. Patrice   L   P-Volume 1

PARISH: 1813 - St. Georges de Cacouna   P-Volume 2

PARISH: 1849 - St. Arsene de Cacouna   P-Volume 2

PARISH: 1852 - St. Eloi   P-Pontbriand & Laliberte, P-Vol 3

PARISH: 1853 - St. Modeste - P-Volume 2

PARISH: 1857 - Notre Dame du Portage   L   P-Volume 1
                        XX-Levesque-Belanger

PARISH: 1858 - St. Antonin   L   P-Volume 1   P-Proulx

PARISH: 1863 - St. Epiphane   P-Volume 2

PARISH: 1864 - Ste. Francoise   P-Volume 3

PARISH: 1871 - St. Francois Xavier de Viger   L   K-Edmond,
                        P-Volume 2

PARISH: 1873 - St. Paul de la Croix   P-Volume 2

PARISH: 1874 - St. Jean de Dieu   P-Volume 3

PARISH: 1875 - St. Clement   P-Volume 3

PARISH: 1876 - Notre Dame des Sept Douleurs de I'lle Verte
                        P-Volume 2

PARISH: 1886 - St. Hubert   P-Volume 2

PARISH: 1888 - St.Cyprien   P-Volume 2

* P- Gingras, Roy & Beaulieu - Volumes 1 & 2

Roy & Beaulieu - Volumes 3 & 4
with Societe Genealogique de L'Est du Quebec

COUNTY: Rouville

LOCATION: South

REFERENCE: Southeast of Montreal

MAP: 7

ARCHIVES: Sherbrooke/Montreal

CITY REFERENCE: Marieville

FIRST PARISH: 1739 - St. Mathias (La Conception Pointe Oliver)
                          L   J-Raymond & Jette

PARISH: 1740 - St. Charles Sur Richelieu   - see St. Hyacinthe

PARISH: 1797 - St. Jean Baptiste de Rouville   L
                 J- Pontbriand & Jette

PARISH: 1799 - St. Hilaire   (Mont St. Hilaire)   L
                 J- Pontbriand & R. Jette

PARISH: 1801 - St. Nom de Marie - Marie de Monnoir
                 (Marieville)   L   J-Jette

PARISH: 1822 - St. Cesaire   (Rouville)   L   J-Jette & Provencher

PARISH: 1856 - St. Paul d'Abbotsford   L   J-Jette & Provencher

PARISH: 1857 - L'Ange Gardien   (Rouville)   L   J-Jette & Provencher

PARISH: 1865 - Ste. Angele de Monnoir   L   J-Jette

PARISH: 1868 - Notre Dame de Bonsecours   (Richelieu)   L
                 J-Raymond & Jette

PARISH: 1886 - St. Michel   (Rougemont)   L   J-Jette & Provencher

COUNTY: Saguenay   (Includes Labrador Peninsula) *

LOCATION: Far North

REFERENCE: Extreme Northeast of Quebec

MAP: 39

ARCHIVES: Sept Isles

CITY REFERENCE: Tadoussac

FIRST PARISH: 1668 - Tadoussac - Postes du Domaine du Roi

PARISH: 1845 - Notre Dame de Betsiamites

PARISH: 1846 - St. Marcellin (Escoumins) Sept Isles P-Vol 1

PARISH: 1858 - St. Pierre de la Point aux Esquimaux (Labrador)
          (Havre St. Pierre) P-Vol 2

PARISH: 1861 - Notre Dame du Natashquan (Labrador) P-Vol 2

PARISH: 1861 - Ste Anne de Saguenay - see Chicoutimi

PARISH: 1863 - Ste. Croix de Tadoussac

PARISH: 1867 - St. Joseph de Moisie   (Mission de la Riviere
          Moisie) (St. Vital) (Labrador) P-Vol 1

PARISH: 1868 - St. Dominique de Jonquiere - see Chicoutimi

PARISH: 1870 - St. Paul du Nord de la Baie de Mille Vaches

PARISH: 1876 - St. Octave de Magpie (Riviere St. Jean)
          (Labrador) P-Vol 2

PARISH: 1876 - St. Joseph (Tabatiere) (Labrador) P- Vol 2

PARISH: 1884 - Sacre Coeur de Jesus (Bonne Esperance) P- 2

PARISH: 1884 - Notre Dame de l'Assomption (Anticosti-Pt. Menier)
          (Labrador) P-Vol 2

PARISH: 1887 - St. Georges (Mingan) (Labrador) P-Vol 2

PARISH: 1888 - Mission Indienne (Musquaro) P-Vol 2

PARISH: 1893 - Immaculee Conception (Blanc Sablon) (Labrador)
          P-Vol 2

PARISH: 1894 - Sacre Coeur (La Romaine) P-Vol 2

PARISH: 1898 - St. Hippolyte (Riviere au Tonnerre) P-Vol 2

*P-Doyle   in Collaboration with Societe Genealogique de l'Est
          du Quebec - also offered by D.D. - 2 Volumes
          Vol-1 Judicial district Sept Isles (Baie Trinite-Sept Iles
          Vol-2 Basse Cote Nord (east of Moisie Riviere to Blanc Sablon)
      X-Talbot   (5Volumes)

COUNTY: Shefford *

LOCATION: South

REFERENCE: Southeast of Montreal

MAP: 42

ARCHIVES: Sherbrooke

CITY REFERENCE: Granby **

FIRST PARISH: 1841 - Mission de Canton de l'Est J-Jette &
Beauregard

PARISH: 1844 - Notre Dame (Granby) L

PARISH: 1846 - Notre Dame de Bonsecours (Stukeley) L

PARISH: 1846 - Ste. Cecile (Milton) L

PARISH: 1850 - St. Jean Baptiste (Roxton Falls) L

PARISH: 1854 - St. Joseph d'Ely (Valcourt)

PARISH: 1854 - St. Valerien (Milton) L

PARISH: 1857 - Ste. Anne de Stukeley (La Rochelle) L

PARISH: 1859 - St. Francois Xavier de West Shefford (Bromont)

PARISH: 1860 - St. Joachim de Shefford

PARISH: 1865 - St. Bernardin (Waterloo) L

PARISH: 1873 - Ste. Prudentienne (Roxton Pond) L

PARISH: 1875 - St. Alphonse (Granby) L

PARISH: 1893 - Ste. Marie d'Ely (Maricourt)

PARISH: 1906 - St. Theophile d'Ely (Racine)

PARISH: 1916 - Enfant Jesus d'Ely (Bethanie)

* J-Pontbriand & Jette (1846-1968)

** J-Pontbriand

COUNTY: Sherbrooke   *

LOCATION: South

REFERENCE: Southeast of Montreal

MAP: 47

ARCHIVES: Sherbrooke

CITY REFERENCE: Sherbrooke

FIRST PARISH: 1834 - Cathedrale St. Michel   (St. Colomban)
                          (Sherbrooke)   L   J-Pare, Pontbriand &
                          Laliberte

PARISH: 1878 - St. Antoine   (Lennoxville)

PARISH: 1884 - St. Jean Baptiste   (Sherbrooke)   L

PARISH: 1886 - St. Elie d'Orford   L

PARISH: 1887 - St. Patrick   (Sherbrooke)

PARISH: 1891 - St. Roch   (Rock Forest)   L   XX-Lambert

PARISH: 1894 - St. Stanislas   (Ascot Corner)

PARISH: 1906 - Precieux Sang   (Capelton)

*   M-Collaboration - 3 Volumes
     F-Campagna

COUNTY: Soulanges *

LOCATION: North

REFERENCE: West of Montreal

MAP: 15

ARCHIVES: Montreal

CITY REFERENCE: Coteau Landing

FIRST PARISH: 1752 - St. Joseph de Soulanges (Les Cedres)
                        F-Charette

PARISH: 1819 - St. Polycarpe L

PARISH: 1833 - St. Ignance du Coteau du Lac F-Charette

PARISH: 1851 - St. Clet L

PARISH: 1852 - St. Zotique

PARISH: 1876 - St. Telesphore L

PARISH: 1895 - St. Medard (Coteau Station) B-Charette

PARISH: 1905 - Ste. Claire de Assise (Riviere Beaudette)

* F-Houle

COUNTY: Stanstead *

LOCATION: Far South

REFERENCE: Southeast of Montreal, near Vermont

MAP: 48

ARCHIVES: Sherbrooke

CITY REFERENCE: Ayer's Cliff

FIRST PARISH: 1848 - Sacre Coeur de Jesus   (Stanstead Plains)
             L C-Jette

PARISH: 1861 - St. Patrice de Magog   C-Jette

PARISH: 1862 - St. Venant de Hereford   (Paquetteville) - see
             Compton

PARISH: 1868 - St. Edmond de Coaticook L C-Jette

PARISH: 1875 - St. Hermengilde (Barford) L C-Jette

PARISH: 1876 - Ste. Suzanne (Stanhope) C-R.Jette

PARISH: 1881 - Ste. Catherine (Katevale) L C-Jette

PARISH: 1904 - St. Wilfred (Kingscroft) L

PARISH: 1908 - St. Elizabeth (North, Hatley)

PARISH: 1913 - St. Jean Evangeliste (Coaticook)

PARISH: 1915 - St. Mathieu (Dixville) C-Jette

PARISH: 1916 - St. Marc (Coaticook)

PARISH: 1916 - Notre Dame de Merci (Rock Island)

PARISH: 1921 - Ste Marguerite Marie (Magog)

PARISH: 1923 - St. Ephrem (Fitch Bay)

PARISH: 1925 - Ste. Therese (Beebe Plain) L C-Jette

* M-Collaboration (2 Volumes)
  F-Campagna

COUNTY: St. Hyacinthe

LOCATION: South

REFERENCE: East of Montreal

MAP: 5

ARCHIVES: Sherbrooke/Montreal

CITY REFERENCE: St. Hyacinthe

FIRST PARISH: 1740 - St. Charles Sur Richelieu L
              J- Pontbriand & Jette

PARISH: 1740 - St. Denis Sur Richelieu L J-Loiselle

PARISH: 1777 - Notre Dames du Rosaire de St. Hyacinthe L
              J-Jette M-Collaboration

PARISH: 1806 - La Presentation L J-Jette M-Collaboration

PARISH: 1822 - St. Jude L J-Jette M-Collaboration XX-Delorme

PARISH: 1823 - St. Damase L J-Pontbriand &Jette

PARISH: 1832 - St. Simon de St. Hyacinthe - see Bagot

PARISH: 1840 - St. Barnabe Sud L J-Jette M-Collaboration

PARISH: 1854 - Cathedrale (St. Hyacinthe Le Confesseur)
              L J-Pontbriand & Jette

PARISH: 1854 - Ste. Helene de St. Hyacinthe - see Bagot

PARISH: 1857 - L'Ange Gardien de St. Hyacinthe - see Rouville

PARISH: 1876 - Ste. Marie Madeleine L J-Pontbriand & Jette

PARISH: 1891 - St. Thomas d'Aquin L J-Jette M-Collaboration

PARISH: 1908 - St. Bernard de Michaudville L J-Jette
              M-Collaboration

PARISH: 1916 - St. Joseph J-Pontbriand & Jette

COUNTY: St. Jean *

LOCATION: South

REFERENCE: South of Montreal

MAP: 9

ARCHIVES: Montreal

CITY REFERENCE: St. Jean

FIRST PARISH: 1739 - La Conception de la Pointe Oliver
                      (St. Mathias) - see Rouville

PARISH: 1757 - Fort St Jean (* with N.D. Montreal or St. Charles
               sur Richelieu)

PARISH: 1784 - Ste. Marguerite de Blairfindie (L'Acadie)
               L   J-Jette & Granger

PARISH: 1801 - St. Luc (Hetres) L   J-Jette & Granger

PARISH: 1813 - Registre Militaire I'lle Aux Noix (with N.D.
               Montreal or St. Charles sur Richelieu)

PARISH: 1828 - St. Jean L'Evangeliste (Cathedrale) (St. Jean
               sur Richelieu) L   F-Lemieux

PARISH: 1830 - St. Valentin L

PARISH: 1833 - St. Georges de Henryville - see Iberville

PARISH: 1839 - Grande Ligne de L'Acadie (Desserte)

PARISH: 1843 - St. Bernard de Lacolle

PARISH: 1887 - St. Blaise

PARISH: 1898 - St. Paul I'le Aux Noix

PARISH: 1902 - Notre Dame du Mt. Carmel (Lacolle)

PARISH: 1906 - Notre Dame Auxilliatrice St. Jean

*J-Jette (2 volumes 1828-1950)

COUNTY: Saint Maurice

LOCATION: North

REFERENCE: at Three Rivers

MAP: 28

ARCHIVES: Three Rivers

CITY REFERENCE: Three Rivers

FIRST PARISH: 1634 - L'Immaculee Conception des Trois Rivieres
                     (Notre Dame de la Conception)
                     L F-Campagna, M-Collaboration (2 Vol)

PARISH: 1718 - Ste Anne de Yamachiche L F-Campagna

PARISH: 1740 - St. Louis de Ville Forges de St. Maurice
                (Forges du St. Maurice) M-Collaboration (2 Vol)

PARISH: 1742 - La Visitation de la Pointe du Lac (Tonnancour)
                L F-Campagna

PARISH: 1796 - Hospital des Ursulines de Trois Rivieres

PARISH: 1833 - St. Barnabe Nord O-St. Cyr

PARISH: 1838 - Christ Roi de Shawinigan (protestant) O -St. Cyr

PARISH: 1856 - St. Severe L O-Pellerin

PARISH: 1857 - St.Etienne des Gres - O-Pellerin & Therrien

PARISH: 1861 - St. Boniface de Shawinigan O-Samson & Gelinas

PARISH: 1865 - Ste. Flore (Grand Mere) - see Champlain

PARISH: 1872 - St. Elie de Caxton O-Blais

PARISH: 1872 - St. Mathieu Lac Bellemare O-Therrien

PARISH: 1899 - Sacre Coeur de Baie Shawinigan O-Collaboration

PARISH: 1899 - Notre Dame Almaville

PARISH: 1899 - St. Pierre de Shawinigan L O-Collaboration

PARISH: 1899 - St. Malo - see Quebec

PARISH: 1900 - St. Michel des Forges O-Grondin & Descoteau

PARISH: 1904 - St. Thomas de Caxton O-Therrien

108

COUNTY: Temiscamingue   *

LOCATION: Far North

REFERENCE: North of Ottawa

MAP: 73

ARCHIVES: Rouyn Noranda

CITY REFERENCE: Ville Marie

FIRST PARISH: 1889 - Notre Dame de Rosarie (Ville Marie)   L

PARISH: 1896 - St. Joseph (Notre Dame du Nord)

PARISH: 1899 - St. Edouard (Fabre)

PARISH: 1905 - St. Bruno (Guigues)

PARISH: 1906 - Notre Dame de Lourdes (Lorrainville)

PARISH: 1907 - St. Placide (Bern)

PARISH: 1911 - St. Isidore (Laverlochere)

PARISH: 1911 - St. Eugene (Guigues)

PARISH: 1912 - Notre Dame du Mt. Carmel (Fugreville)

PARISH: 1912 - St. Gabriel (Guerin)

PARISH: 1912 - St. Antoine Abbe (La Tulippe)

PARISH: 1914 - St. Louis de France (Nedelec)

PARISH: 1925 - St. Michael Archange (Rouyn)

* M-Collaboration, F-Fournier, Hamelin & Houle

COUNTY: Temiscouata *

LOCATION: Gaspe

REFERENCE: South of Riviere du Loup, near Maine & New Brunswick

MAP: 64

ARCHIVES: Quebec

CITY REFERENCE: Notre Dame du Lac

FIRST PARISH: 1713 - Notre Dame des Neiges (Trois Pistoles)
see Riviere du Loup

PARISH: 1766 - St. Jean Baptiste (Ile Verte) - see Riviere du Loup

PARISH: 1853 - St. Modeste   - see Riviere du Loup

PARISH: 1858 - St. Antonin - see Riviere du Loup

PARISH: 1861 - Notre Dame du Lac P- Volume 4

PARISH: 1863 - St. Epiphane   - see Riviere du Loup

PARISH: 1864 - Ste. Francoise - see Riviere du Loup

PARISH: 1871 - St. Honore P- Volume 4

PARISH: 1873 - St. Paul de la Croix   - see Riviere du Loup

PARISH: 1874 - St. Jean de Dieu - see Riviere du Loup

PARISH: 1875 - St. Clement - see Riviere du Loup

PARISH: 1876 - Notre Dame des Sept Douleurs - see Riviere du Loup

PARISH: 1877 - Ste. Rose de Degele   P-Volume 4

PARISH: 1878 - St. Louis du Ha!Ha! P- Volume 4

PARISH: 1886 - St. Hubert - see Riviere du Loup

PARISH: 1918 - St. David d'Estcourt (Sully)

PARISH: 1929 - Ste. Marie Mediatrice d'Estcourt

* P - Gingras, Roy & Beaulieu - Volumes 1 & 2
    Roy & Beaulieu - Volumes 3 & 4
    with Societe Genealogique de L'Est du Quebec

COUNTY: Terrebonne *

LOCATION: North

REFERENCE: North of Montreal

MAP: 23

ARCHIVES: Montreal

CITY REFERENCE: St. Jerome

FIRST PARISH: 1725 - St. Louis de Terrebonne   L   R   C-Gauthier &
                        Bergeron   T-Collaboration

PARISH: 1788 - Ste. Anne des Plaines   L   R   T-Collaboration

PARISH: 1789 - Ste. Therese de Blainville   L   R   C-Collaboration
                    T-Collaboration

PARISH: 1837 - St. Jerome (Cathedrale)   L   R   C-Laliberte

PARISH: 1846 - St. Janvier de Blainville (Mirabel)
                    L   R   T-Laliberte

PARISH: 1851 - Ste. Sophie   L   R   T-Laliberte

PARISH: 1852 - Ste. Adele   L   R   T-Laliberte

PARISH: 1853 - St. Sauveur des Monts   L   R   T-Laliberte

PARISH: 1861 - Ste. Agathe des Monts   R   T-Laliberte

PARISH: 1866 - St. Hippolyte de Kilkenny   L   R   T-Laliberte

PARISH: 1866 - Ste. Marguerite du Lac Masson   R   T-Laliberte

PARISH: 1878 - Ste. Lucie (Laurentides)   R   **

PARISH: 1879 - St. Jovite (Laurentides)   R   **

PARISH: 1886 - St. Faustin (Laurentides)   L   R   **

PARISH: 1894 - St. Agricole

* TT.-Rivest (10 Volumes)

** T-Lavoie (1940-1984)

COUNTY: Vaudreuil

LOCATION: North

REFERENCE: West of Montreal

MAP: 16

ARCHIVES: Montreal

CITY REFERENCE: Vaudreuil

FIRST PARISH: 1773 - St. Michel Vaudreuil L F-Charette,

PARISH: 1786 - Ste. Jeanne de Chantal de I'lle Perrot C-Legault

PARISH: 1802 - Ste. Madeleine de Rigaud F-Charette

PARISH: 1844 - Ste. Marthe F-Hamelin

PARISH: 1865 - Ste. Justine de Newton F-Campagna & Hamelin

PARISH: 1875 - St. Lazare F-Campagna & Hamelin

PARISH: 1880 - Tres Saint Redempteur (Dorion) F-Campagna & Hamelin

PARISH: 1897 - St. Thomas d'Aquin (Hudson) F-Campagna & Hamelin

COUNTY: Vercheres

LOCATION: South

REFERENCE: East of Montreal

MAP: 4

ARCHIVES: Montreal

CITY REFERENCE: Vercheres

FIRST PARISH: 1681 - Tres St. Trinite de Contrecoeur   L   J-Jette

PARISH: 1693 - Ste. Anne de Varennes   L   J-Jette & Pontbriand

PARISH: 1724 - St. Francois Xavier de Vercheres   L   J-Jette

PARISH: 1741 - St. Denis Sur Richelieu - see St. Hyacinthe

PARISH: 1741 - St. Antoine Sur Richelieu
                (St. Antoine de Chambly)   L   J-Jette

PARISH: 1772 - St. Mathieu de Beloeil   J-Jette

PARISH: 1794 - St. Marc de Cournoyer sur Richelieu   L   J-Jette

PARISH: 1852 - Ste. Julie de Vercheres   J-Jette

PARISH: 1859 - St. Roch Sur Richelieu - see Richelieu

PARISH: 1880 - Ste. Theodosie (Calixa Lavalee)   J-Jette

PARISH: 1913 - St. Amable de Vercheres   J-Jette

COUNTY: Wolfe   *

LOCATION: South

REFERENCE: Southwest of Quebec

MAP: 51

ARCHIVES: Sherbrooke

CITY REFERENCE: Ham Sud

FIRST PARISH: 1851 - St. Hippolyte   (Wotton)   L

PARISH: 1857 - St. Gabriel de Stratford Centre   L

PARISH: 1863 - St. Janvier de Weedon   L

PARISH: 1864 - St. Julien   (Wolfestown)   L

PARISH: 1865 - Tres Sts. Anges   (Ham Nord)

PARISH: 1868 - St. Camille   (Wotton)   L

PARISH: 1876 - St. Fortunat de Wolfestown

PARISH: 1876 - St. Charles Borromee (St. Oliver)   (Garthby)

PARISH: 1883 - St. Joseph de Ham Sud

PARISH: 1886 - St. Adrien de Ham

PARISH: 1887 - St. Adolphe de Dudswell

PARISH: 1894 - St. Luc   (Disraeli)

PARISH: 1897 - Notre Dame de Lourdes   (Massabielle)

*   M-Collaboration - 3 Volumes
    F-Campagna

COUNTY: Yamaska

LOCATION: South

REFERENCE:Southwest of Three Rivers

MAP: 44

ARCHIVES: Three Rivers

CITY REFERENCE: St. Francois du Lac

FIRST PARISH: 1687 - St. Francois du Lac   L R   J-Mongeau &
                    Laliberte

PARISH: 1715 - St. Antoine de la Baie de Febvre   L R J-Mongeau

PARISH: 1727 - St. Michel d'Yamaska   L R J-Laliberte, Mongeau &
                    Pontbriand

PARISH: 1835 - St. David de Guire   L R J-Laliberte, Mongeau &
                    Pontbriand

PARISH: 1835 - St. Guillaume d'Upton - see Drummond

PARISH: 1846 - St. Zephirin de Courval   L R   J-Partenteau,
                .   Laliberte & Pontbriand

PARISH: 1848 - Mission des Abenaquis & Socoquis (Odanak)   L R
                    J- Mongeau & Laliberte (Catholic & Protestant)

PARISH: 1848 - Mission St. Francois de Sales   (Riviere St.
                    Francois)

PARISH: 1853 - St. Thomas de Pierreville   L R   J-Mongeau &
                    Laliberte

PARISH: 1866   St. Bonaventure d'Upton - see Drummond

PARISH: 1874 - St. Pie de Guire   L R J-Partenteau, Laliberte
                    & Pontbriand

PARISH: 1886 - St. Elphegie   R   J-Partenteau, Laliberte &
                    Pontbriand

PARISH: 1893 - Notre Dame de Pierreville   L R   J-Mongeau &
                    Laliberte

PARISH: 1898 - La Visitation de BVM   R J-Partenteau, Laliberte
                    & Pontbriand

PARISH: 1901 - St. Joachim de Courval   R J-Partenteau, Laliberte
                    & Pontbriand

INDEX TO COUNTIES

Hochlega	North	Montreal	Montreal	57
Hull	North	Hull	Hull	54
Huntingdon	Far South	Montreal	Huntingdon	55
Iberville	South	Sherbrooke	Iberville	56
I'lle Jesus	North	Montreal	Laval	68
I'lle Montreal	North	Montreal	Montreal	57
Iles de la Madeleine	Off Gaspe	Rimouski	Havre aux Maisons	60
Jacques Cartier	North	Montreal	Montreal	57
Joliette	North	Montreal	Joliette	61
Kamouraska	South	Quebec	St. Pascal	62
Labelle	North	Hull/Montreal	Mont Laurier	63
Lac St. Jean Est	Far North	Chicoutimi	Alma	64
Lac St. Jean Quest	Far North	Chicoutimi	Roberval	65
Laprairie	South	Montreal	Laprairie	66
L'Assomption	North	Montreal	L'Assomption	67
Laval	North	Montreal	Montreal	68
Levis	South	Quebec	St. Romuald	69
L'Islet	South	Quebec	St. Jean Port Joli	70
Lotbiniere	South	Quebec	Ste. Croix	71
Maskinonge	North	Three Rivers	Louisville	73
Matane	Gaspe	Rimouski	Matane	74
Matapedia	Gaspe	Rimouski	Amqui	75
Megantic	South	Quebec	Inverness	76
Missisquoi	Far South	Sherbrooke	Bedford	77
Montcalm	North	Montreal	Ste. Julienne	78
Montmagny	South	Quebec	Montmagny	79
Montmorency #1	North	Quebec	Chateau Richer	80
Montmorency #2	North	Quebec	Ile de Orleans	81

118

Napierville	South	Montreal	Napierville	82
Nicolet	South	Three Rivers	Becancour	83
Ottawa	Ontario	Ottawa	Ottawa	84
Papineau	North	Hull	Papineauville	86
Pontiac	North	Hull	Campbell's Bay	88
Portneuf	North	Quebec	Cap Sante	89
Quebec	North	Quebec	Quebec	91
Richelieu	South	Shrbrke/Mtrl	Sorel	93
Richmond	South	Sherbrooke	Richmond	94
Rimouski	Gaspe	Rimouski	Rimouski	95
Riviere du Loup	South	Quebec	Riviere du Loup	97
Rouville	South	Shrbrke/Mtrl	Marieville	99
Saguenay	Far North	Sept Iles	Tadoussac	100
Shefford	South	Sherbrooke	Granby	102
Sherbrooke	South	Sherbrooke	Sherbrooke	103
Soulanges	North	Montreal	Coteau Landing	104
Stanstead	Far South	Sherbrooke	Ayer's Cliff	105
St. Hyacinthe	South	Shrbrke/Mtrl	St. Hyacinthe	106
St. Jean	South	Montreal	St. Jean	107
St. Maurice	North	Three Rivers	Three Rivers	108
Temiscamingue	Far North	Rouyn/Noranda	Ville Marie	109
Temiscouata	Gaspe	Quebec	Notre Dame du Lac	110
Terrebonne	North	Montreal	St. Jerome	111
Vaudreuil	North	Montreal	Vaudreuil	112
Vercheres	South	Montreal	Vercheres	113
Wolfe	South	Quebec	Ham Sud	114
Yamaska	South	Three Rivers	St. Francois du Lac	115

INDEX TO PARISHES

121

Bromont	Shefford
Bromptonville	Richmond
Buckingham	Papineau
Bury	Compton
Caldwell & Christie Maners	Iberville
Caplan	Bonaventure
Cap-Chat	Gaspe West
Cap-de-la-Madeleine	Champlain
Cap -d'Espoir	Gaspe East
Cap des Rosiers	Gaspe East
Cap Rouge	Quebec
Cap Sante	Portneuf
Cap St. Ignance	Montmagny
Carleton	Bonaventure
Cascapedia	Bonaventure
Cathedrale - Mont Laurier	Labelle
Cathedrale	St. Hyacinthe
Cathedrale St. Michel	Sherbrooke
Causapscal	Matapedia
Chambly	Chambly
Chambord	Lac St.Jean Est
Champlain	Champlain
Chapeau	Pontiac
Charlesbourg	Quebec
Chartierville	Compton
Chateauguay	Chateauguay
Chateau Richer	Montmorency #1
Chatham	Argeuntil
Chatham - Protestant	Argeuntil
Cheneville	Papineau
Chicoutimi	Chicoutimi
Chicoutimi - Nord	Chicoutimi
Christ Church - Sorel	Richelieu
Christieville	Iberville
Christ Roi (Cathedrale)	Gaspe
Christ Roi de Shawinigan	St. Maurice
Clarence Creek	Ottawa
Cloridorme	Gaspe East
Coaticook	Stanstead
Compton	Compton
Contrecoeur	Vercheres
Cookshire	Compton
Coteau du Lac	Soulanges
Cowansville	Missisquoi
Curran	Ottawa
Dalesville	Argenteuil
Danville	Richmond
Deschaillons	Lotbiniere
Deschambault	Portneuf
Donnacona	Portneuf
Dorval	I'lle Montreal
Douglastown	Gaspe East
Drummondville	Drummond
Duhamel	Papineau
Dundee	Huntingdon

Dunham	Missisquoi
Dupuy	Abitibi
Durham - Sud	Drummond
East Broughton	Beauce
Eastman	Brome
Eboulements	Charlevoix Quest
Enfant Jesus	Beauce
Enfant Jesus d'Ely - Bethanie	Shefford
Escoumins	Saguenay
Farnham	Missisquoi
Ferme Neuve	LaBelle
Forges du St. Maurice	St. Maurice
Fort Lorette	I'lle Montreal
Fort St Jean	St. Jean
Franklin	Huntingdon
Fugreville	Temiscamingue
Gaspe	Gaspe East
Gaspe - Cap des Rosiers	Gaspe East
Gaspe - Douglastown	Gaspe East
Gaspe - Riviere au Renard	Gaspe East
Gatineau - Cantely	Gatineau
Gatineau - Pointe Gatineau	Hull
Gentilly	Nicolet
Gesu (Montreal)	I'lle Montreal
Gracefield	Gatineau
Granby	Shefford
Grand-Calumet	Pontiac
Grande Baie	Chicoutimi
Grande Riviere	Gaspe East
Grand Mere	Champlain
Grand Vallee	Gaspe East
Grenville	Argenteuil
Grondines	Portneuf
Grosse Ile	Iles de la Madeleine
Grosses Roches	Matane
Ham- Nord	Wolfe
Havre Aubert	Iles de la Madeleine
Havre aux Maisons	Iles de la Madeleine
Havre St. Pierre	Saguenay
Hebertville	Lac St. Jean Est
Hemmingford	Huntingdon
Henryville	Iberville
Hinchinbrooke - Athelstan	Huntingdon
Holy Trinity	Iles de la Madeleine
Hopital de la Marine	Quebec
Hopital de la Misericorde	Ile Jesus
Hopital des Ursulines	St. Maurice
Hopital General de Montreal	I'lle Montreal
Hopital General de Quebec	Quebec
Hospice St. Joseph (Montreal)	I'lle Montreal
Hotel Dieu de Montreal	I'lle Montreal
Hotel Dieu de Quebec	Quebec
Huberdeau	Argenteuil
Hull	Hull
Hull Quest - Chelsea	Pontiac

123

Huntingdon	Huntingdon
Iberville	Iberville
Ile aux Noix	St. Jean
Ile du Havre Aubert	Iles de la Madeleine
Ile Dupas	Berthier
Ile Perce	Gaspe East
Ile Perrot	Soulanges
Immaculee Conception	Beauharnois
Immaculee Conception	I'lle Montreal
Immaculee Conception - Blanc Sablon	Saguenay
Inverness	Megantic
Isle aux Coudres	Charlevoix Ouest
Issoudan	Lotbiniere
Joliette	Joliette
Kahnawake	LaPrairie
Kamouraska	Kamouraska
Kiamika	Labelle
Kingsey	Drummond
Kingsey Falls	Arthabaska
Knowlton	Brome
La Baie - Bagotville	Chicoutimi
La Baie - Grande Baie	Chicoutimi
L'Acadie	St. Jean
La Cathedrale	Ottawa
Lac au Saumon	Matapedia
Lac Brome - Knowlton	Brome
Lac des Deux Montagnes	Deux Montagnes
Lac des Ecorces	LaBelle
Lac Etchemin	Dorchester
Lachenaie	L'Assomption
Lachine	I'lle Montreal
Lac Humqui	Matapedia
Lachute	Argenteuil
La Conception	Labelle
La Conception - Pointe Oliver	Rouville
La Decollation de St. Jean Baptiste	Compton
Lac Ste. Marie	Gatineau
La Malbaie	Charlevoix Est
Lambton	Beauce
La Motte	Abitibi
La Nativite de la B.V.M.	Nicolet
La Nativite de la B.V.M.	Laprairie
La Nativite de la B.V.M. - Hochlega	I'lle Montreal
La Nativite de N. D. - Beauport	Quebec
La Nativite de N. D.- Becancour	Nicolet
L'Ancienne Lorette	Quebec
Landrienne	Abitibi
L'Ange Gardien	Montmorency #1
L'Ange Gardien	Rouville
L'Ange Gardien d'Angers	Ottawa
L'Annonciation	Deux Montagnes
L'Annonciation	Labelle
Lanoraie	Berthier
L'Anse	St. Jean
La Patrie	Compton

124

La Peche	Gatineau
La Peche - Farrellton	Gatineau
La Perade	Champlain
La Pocatiere	Kamouraska
Laprairie	LaPrairie
La Presentation de la Ste. Vierge	I'lle Montreal
La Presentation	St. Hyacinthe
La Purification de la B.V.M	L'Assomption
La Reine	Abitibi
La Sarre	Abitibi
L'Assomption	L'Assomption
L'Assomption de la B.V.M.	L'Assomption
L'Assomption de la Ste. Vierge	Charlevoix Quest
L'Assomption de Notre Dame	Gaspe East
L'Assomption de N.D. - McNider	Matane
Laterriere	Chicoutimi
La Tuque	Champlain
Laurentides	L'Assomption
Laurierville	Megantic
Lauzon	Levis
Laval - Chomedey	I'lle Jesus
Laval - Ste. Dorothee	I'lle Jesus
Laval - Ste. Rose	I'lle Jesus
Laval - St. Francois	I'lle Jesus
Laval - St. Vincent de Paul	I'lle Jesus
Lavaltrie	Berthier
L'Avenir	Drummond
La Visitation - Pointe du Lac	St. Maurice
La Visitation	Yamaska
La Visitation de la Gatineau	Gatineau
La Visitation de Ottawa	Ottawa
La V. de la Ste. V.M.-I'le Dupas	Berthier
La V. de N.D. - Gracefield	Gatineau
La V. de N.D. - Chateau Richer	Montmorency #1
La Visitation - Sault au Recollet	I'lle Montreal
Le Gardeur	L'Assomption
Leclercville	Lotbiniere
L'Enfant Jesus - Pt. aux Trembles	I'lle Montreal
Lennoxville	Sherbrooke
L'Epiphanie	L'Assomption
Les Becquets	Nicolet
Les Cedres	Soulanges
Les Eboulements	Charlevoix Quest
Les Ecureuils	Portneuf
Les Escoumins	Saguenay
Levis	Levis
L'Ile Verte	Riviere du Loup
L'Immaculee Conception de St.Ours	Richelieu
L'Immaculee Conception	St. Maurice
Liniere	Beauce
L'Islet	L'Islet
Litchfield - Vinton	Pontiac
Longueuil	Chambly
Longue Pointe	I'lle Jesus
Loretteville (Mission des Hurons)	Quebec

Loretteville - St. Ambroise	Quebec
L'Original	Ottawa
Lotbiniere	Lotbiniere
Louiseville	Maskinonge
Luskville	Gatineau
Lyster	Megantic
Magog	Stanstead
Magpie	Saguenay
Maniwaki	Gatineau
Mansonville	Brome
Mantawa	Joliette
Maria	Bonaventure
Marie Reine du Monde	Montcalm
Marieville	Rouville
Martindale	Gatineau
Mascouche	L'Assomption
Maskinonge	Maskinonge
Masson - Angers	Papineau
Massueville	Rouville
Matane	Matane
Mercier	Chateauguay
Metabetchouan	Lac St. Jean Est
Mille Vaches	Saguenay
Mirabel	Deux Montagnes
Mission de Buckingham	Papineau
Mission de Causapscal	Matapedia
Mission de Fort William - Sheenboro	Pontiac
Mission de la Montagne	I'lle Montreal
Mission de I'lle aux Tortes	Deux Montagnes
Mission des Abenaquis de St. F.de S.	Yamaska
Mission des Abenaquis et Socoquis	Yamaska
Mission des Cantons de Est	Shefford
Mission des Hurons	Quebec
Mission Indienne - Musquaro	Saguenay
Mission de l'Intercolonial	Matapedia
Mission de St. Edouard les Mechins	Matane
Mission de St. Joseph de Sillery	Quebec
Mission de Warmontashing	Gatineau
Mission du Canton de Shipton	Richmond
Mission Notre Dame des Neiges	I'lle Montreal
Mission St. Cajetan	Gatineau
Mission St. Francois de Sales	Yamaska
Mission St. Louis	Deux Montagnes
Mistassini - James Bay	Lac St. Jean Quest
Moisie	Saguenay
Mont Carmel	Kamouraska
Montcerf	Gatineau
Montebello	Papineau
Montfort	Argenteuil
Mont Joli	Rimouski
Mont Louis	Gaspe West
Montmagny	Montmagny
Montminy	Montmagny
Montreal	I'lle Montreal
Mont St. Gregorie	Iberville

Mont St. Hilaire	Rouville
Napierville	Napierville
Natashquan	Saguenay
Nedelec	Temiscaminque
Neuville	Portneuf
New Richmond	Bonaventure
Newport	Gaspe East
Nicolet	Nicolet
Nomininque	Labelle
Norbertville	Arthabaska
Normandin	Lac St. Jean Quest
Notre Dame - Almaville	St. Maurice
Notre Dame Auxiliatrice	St. Jean
N.D. Auxiliatrice des Montagnes	Bellechasse
Notre Dame de Bellerive	Beauharnois
Notre Dame de Betsiamites	Saguenay
Notre Dame de Bon Conseil	Drummond
Notre Dame de Bon Conseil	Ottawa
Notre Dame de Bonsecours	L'Islet
Notre Dame de Bonsecours	Ottawa
N.D. de Bonsecours - Montebello	Papineau
Notre Dame de Bonsecours	Rouville
N.D. de Bonsecours de Stukely	Shefford
Notre Dame de Foy	Quebec
Notre Dame de Grace	Hull
Notre Dame de Grace	I'lle Montreal
Notre Dame de Granby	Shefford
Notre Dame de Grande Riviere	Gaspe East
Notre Dame de Jacques Cartier	Quebec
Notre Dame de la Consolation	Papineau
Notre Dame de la Garde - Val des Bois	Papineau
Notre Dame de la Garde	Quebec
N.D. de l'Annonciation	Quebec
N.D. de la Merci	Montcalm
Notre Dame de la Paix	Papineau
Notre Dame de la Salette	Papineau
N.D. de l'Assomption	Saguenay
N.D. de l'Assomption	Matane
N.D. de l'Assomption Bellechasse	Montmagny
N.D. de l'Assomption de Maniwaki	Gatineau
Notre Dame de Laus	LaBelle
Notre Dame de la Purification	Bonaventure
N.D. de la Victorie	Levis
N.D. de la Visitation	Iles de la Madeleine
Notre Dame de la Visitation	Champlain
Notre Dame de la Visitation	Montmorency #1
Notre Dame de Liesse	Kamouraska
N.D. de l'Immaculee Conception	Chicoutimi
Notre Dame de l'Immaculle Conception	Quebec
Notre Dame de Lorette	I'lle Montreal
Notre Dame de Lorette-Ville des Hurons	Quebec
Notre Dame de Lourdes	Rimouski
Notre Dame de Lourdes	Megantic
Notre Dame de Lourdes - Cyrville	Ottawa
Notre Dame de Lourdes - Lorrainville	Temiscaminque

Notre Dame de Lourdes - Missabielle	Wolfe
Notre Dame de Lourdes - St. Armand	Missisquoi
Notre Dame de Luminiers - Mayo	Papineau
Notre Dame de Merci - Rock Island	Stanstead
Notre Dame de Montreal	I'lle Montreal
Notre Dame de Ottawa	Ottawa
Notre Dame de Paspebiac	Bonaventure
Notre Dame de Perpetule Secours	Richelieu
Notre Dame de Pontmain	Labelle
Notre Dame de Quebec	Quebec
Notre Dame de Pierreville	Yamaska
Notre Dame de Rosarie - Ville Marie	Temiscamingue
Notre Dame de Sacre Coeur	Rimouski
Notre Dame des Anges	Quebec
Notre Dame des Anges	Missisquoi
Notre Dame des Anges - Montauban	Portneuf
Notre Dame des Bois	Frontenac
N.D. des Neiges - Trois Pistoles	Riviere du Loup
N.D. des Sept Douleurs - Grenville	Argenteuil
N.D. des Sept Douleurs - Verdun	I'lle montreal
N.D. des Sept Douleurs-I'lle Verte	Riviere du Loup
N.D. des Sept Douleurs	Portneuf
Notre Dame de Stanbridge	Missisquoi
Notre Dame d'Hebertville	Lac St. Jean Est
Notre Dame du Lac - Roberval	Lac St. Jean Quest
Notre Dame du Lac	Temiscouata
Notre Dame du Las	Labelle
Notre Dame du Mt. Carmel - Lacolle	St. Jean
Notre Dame du Mont Carmel - Valmont	Champlain
Notre Dame du Mont Carmel	Bonaventure
Notre Dame du Mont Carmel	Kamouraska
Notre Dame du Mt. Carmel - Duhamel	Papineau
Notre Dame du Mt. Carmel	Temiscamingue
Notre Dame du Natashquan	Saguenay
Notre Dame du Portage	Riviere du Loup
Notre Dame du Rosaire	I'lle Montreal
Notre Dame du Rosaire	Montmagny
Notre Dame du Rosaire	St. Hyacinthe
N. D. du Sacre Coeur	Rimouski
Notre Dame du Sacre Coeur	Quebec
N. D. du St. Rosarie - Sawyerville	Compton
Nouvelle	Bonaventure
Odanak	Yamaska
Oka	Deux Montagnes
Orleans	Ottawa
Ormstown	Chateauguay
Otter Lake - Leslie	Pontiac
Our Lady of Good Consel	I'lle Montreal
Our Lady of Mt. Carmel - LaPasse	Pontiac
Pabos - Ste. Adelaide	Gaspe East
Pabos - Ste. Famille	Gaspe East
Padoue	Matapedia
Papineauville	Papineau
Paquetteville	Compton
Paspebiac	Bonaventure

128

Pembroke	Ontario/Pontiac
Perce - Barachois	Gaspe East
Perce - Cap d'Espoir	Gaspe East
Perce - I'lle Percee	Gaspe East
Perce - St. Georges de Malbaie	Gaspe East
Perce - St. Michel	Gaspe East
Perkins	Papineau
Petite Nation	Papineau
Petite Riviere	Charlevoix Quest
Pierrefonds	I'lle Montreal
Pierreville	Yamaska
Plaisance	Papineau
Plessisville	Megantic
Pohenegamook	Kamouraska
Pte. aux Chenes	Argenteuil
Pte. aux Esquimaux	Saguenay
Pte. aux Trembles	I'lle Montreal
Pointe Claire	I'lle Montreal
Pointe Levy	Levis
Pointe du Lac	St. Maurice
Pointe Oliver	Rouville
Pointe St. Charles	I'lle Montreal
Pontiac - North Onslow	Pontiac
Pont Rouge	Portneuf
Portage du Fort	Pontiac
Port Daniel	Bonaventure
Portneuf	Portneuf
Postes du Domaine du Roi	Saguenay
Princeville	Arthabaska
Quebec	Quebec
Rawdon	Montcalm
Reg. militaire de I'lle aux Noix	St. Jean
Repentigny	L'Assomption
Restigouche	Bonaventure
Richelieu	Rouville
Richmond	Richmond
Rigaud	Vaudreuil
Rimouski - N.D. Sacre Coeur	Rimouski
Rimouski - St. Germain	Rimouski
Ripon	Papineau
Ristigouche	Bonaventure
Riviere au Rat - Grand 'Anse	Champlain
Riviere au Renard	Gaspe East
Riviere Blanche	Matane
Riviere des Praries	I'lle Montreal
Riviere du Loup	Maskinonge
Riviere du Loup	Temiscouata
Riviere Quelle	Kamouraska
Riviere St. Jean	Saguenay
Robervale	Lac St. Jean Quest
Rockland	Ottawa
Roxton Falls	Shefford
Roxton Pond	Shefford
Sabrevois	Iberville
Sacre Coeur - Grande Entree	Iles de la Madeleine

Sacre Coeur	Ottawa
Sacre Coeur - LaRomaine	Saguenay
Sacre Coeur de Baie Shawinigan	St. Maurice
Sacre Coeur de Jesus - Bonne Esperance	Saguenay
Sacre Coeur de Jesus E. Broughton	Beauce
Sacre Coeur de Jesus - Montreal	I'lle Montreal
Sacre Coeur de Jesus	Stanstead
Sacre Coeur de Jesus - Valleyfield	Beauharnois
Sacre Coeur de Marie - Thetford Mission	Megantic
Salaberry de Valleyfield	Beauharnois
Sault au Recollet	I'lle Montreal
Sault St. Louis	LaPrairie
Sayabec	Matapedia
Senneterre	Abitibi
Sheenboro	Pontiac
Shenley	Beauce
Sherbrooke	Sherbrooke
Sillery - Mission St. Joseph	Quebec
Sillery - St. Colomb	Quebec
Sorel	Richelieu
Stanstead	Stanstead
Stoke	Richmond
Stoneham et Tewkesbury	Quebec
Stratford	Wolfe
Sutton	Brome
St. Adalbert	L'Islet
St. Adelphe	Champlain
St. Adolphe de Dudswell	Wolfe
St. Adolphe de Howard	Argenteuil
St. Adrien de Ham	Wolfe
St. Adrien d'Irlande	Megantic
St. Agricole	Terrebonne
St. Agapit de Beaurivage	Lotbiniere
St. Aime	Richelieu
St. Aime - Asbestos	Richmond
St. Aime de Kingsey Falls	Drummond
St, Alban de Deschambault	Portneuf
St. Alban - Cap des Rosiers	Gaspe East
St. Albert	Gaspe East
St. Albert - Warwick	Arthabaska
St. Alexandre	Kamouraska
St. Alexandre	Iberville
St. Alexander Charteris - Clarendon	Pontiac
St. Alexis	Montcalm
St. Alexis de Grande Baie	Chicoutimi
St. Alexis	Matapedia
St. Alexis des Monts	Maskinonge
St. Alphonse - Thetford Mines	Megantic
St. Alphonse de Granby	Shefford
St. Alphonse de la Grande Baie	Chicoutimi
St. Alphonse - Allumettes	Pontiac
St. Alphonse de Rodriguez	Joliette
St. Alphonse Marie de Liguori	Shefford
St. Alphonsus of Liguori	Pontiac
St. Amable	Vercheres

St. Ambroise de Kildare	Joliette
St. Ambroise de la Jeune	Quebec
St. Anclet de Lessard	Rimouski
St. Andre	Kamouraska
St. Andre - LaSarre	Abitibi
St. Andre - Chambord	Lac St. Jean Ouest
St. Andre Avellin	Papineau
St. Andre d'Acton	Bagot
St. Andre	Argenteuil
St. Andre de Sutton	Brome
St. Andrews East	Argenteuil
St. Ange Gardien	Rouville
St. Anicet	Huntingdon
St. Anselme de Lauzon	Dorchester
St. Anthony	I'lle Montreal
St. Antoine	Vercheres
St. Antoine	Matapedia
St. Antoine	Sherbrooke
St. Antoine Abbe	Huntingdon
St. Antoine Abbe - La Tulipe	Temiscamingue
St. Antoine de Baie de Febvre	Yamaska
St. Antoine de Bienville	Levis
St. Antoine de Pontbriand	Megantic
St. Antoine de Riviere du Loup	Maskinonge
St. Antoine de Lavaltrie	Berthier
St. Antoine de I'lle aux Grues	Montmagny
St. Antoine de Longueuil	Chambly
St. Antoine de Padoue	Maskinonge
St. Antoine de Padoue	Vercheres
St. Antoine de Padoue	Yamaska
St. Antoine de Tilly	Lotbiniere
St. Antoine sur Richelieu	Vercheres
St. Antonin	Riviere du Loup
St. Apollinaire	Lotbiniere
St. Armand - Quest	Missisquoi
St. Arsene	I'lle Montreal
St. Arsene de Cacouna	Riviere du Loup
St. Athanase de Bleury	Iberville
St. Athanase d'Invernoss	Megantic
St. Aubert	L'Islet
St. Augustin	Portneuf
St. Augustin - Woburn	Frontenac
St. Augustin de Desmaures	Portneuf
St. Augustin	Deux Montagnes
St. Barnabe - Landrienne	Abitibi
St. Barnabe Nord	St. Maurice
St. Barnabe Sud	St. Hyacinthe
St. Barthelemy	Berthier
St. Basile	Portneuf
St. Basile le Grand	Chambly
St. Benoit	Deux Montagnes
St. Benoit de Lac	Brome
St. Benoit Joseph Labre	I'lle Montreal
St. Benoit Joseph Labre d'Amqui	Matapedia
St. Benoit Labre	Beauce

St. Bernard	Dorchester
St. Bernard de Lacolle	St. Jean
St. Bernard de Michaudville	St. Hyacinthe
St. Bernardin - Riviere a Pierre	Portneuf
St. Bernardin de Waterloo	Shefford
St. Blaise Grande Ligne	St. Jean
St. Bonaventure de Hamilton	Bonaventure
St. Bonaventure d'Upton	Drummond
St. Boniface de Shawinigan	St. Maurice
St. Bruno	Kamouraska
St. Bruno	Lac St. Jean Est
St. Bruno	Temiscamingue
St. Bruno de Montarville	Chambly
St. Cajetan - Armagh	Bellechasse
St. Calixte	Montcalm
St. Calixte de Somerset	Megantic
St. Camille	Wolfe
St. Camille de Cookshire	Compton
St. Camille de Lellis	Compton
St. Camillus of Farrellton	Gatineau
St. Canut	Deux Montagnes
St. Casimir	Portneuf
St. Casimir de Ripon	Papineau
St. Celestin	Nicolet
St. Cesaire	Rouville
St. Charles	Bellechasse
St. Charles Borromee - Pointe Bleue	Lac St. Jean Quest
St. Charles Borromee	Quebec
St. Charles Borromee - Garthby	Wolfe
St. Charles Borromee de l'Industrie	Joliette
St. Charles de Caplan	Bonaventure
St. Charles de Charlesbourg	Quebec
St. Charles de Lachenaie	L'Assomption
St. Charles - Limoilou	Quebec
St. Charles des Roches	Portneuf
St. Charles sur Richelieu	St. Hyacinthe
St. Christophe	Arthabaska
St. Christophe - I'le Jesus	Laval
St. Chrysostome	Chateauguay
St. Claude	Richmond
St. Clement	Riviere de Loup
St. Clement	Beauharnois
St. Clement - Viauville	I'lle Montreal
St. Cleophas	Joliette
St. Clet	Soulanges
St. Coeur de Marie	Lac St. Jean Est
St. Colomban	Deux Montagnes
St. Colomban	Sherbrooke
St. Colomb de Sillery	Quebec
St. Columbkille	Ontario/Pontiac
St. Come	Joliette
St. Come de Kennebec	Beauce
St. Constant	Laprairie
St. Cuthbert	Berthier
St. Cyprien	Riviere du Loup

St. Cyprien de Lery	Napierville
St. Cyrille de Lessard	L'Islet
St. Cyrille de Wendover	Drummond
St. Damase	Matapedia
St. Damase	St. Hyacinthe
St. Damase des Aulnaies	L'Islet
St. Damien	Bellechasse
St. Damien de Bedford	Missisquoi
St. Damien de Brandon	Berthier
St. David d'Estcourt	Temiscouata
St. David de l'Aube Riviere	Levis
St. David	Yamaska
St. Denis	I'lle Montreal
St. Denis de la Bouteillerie	Kamouraska
St. Denis sur Richelieu	St. Hyacinthe
St. Desire du Lac Noir - Black Lake	Megantic
St. Didace	Maskinonge
St. Dominique	Bagot
St. Dominique d'Eardley	Gatineau
St. Dominique de Jonquiere	Chicoutimi
St. Dominique de Newport	Gaspe East
St. Donat	Montcalm
St. Donat	Rimouski
St. Dunstan du Lac Beauport	Quebec
St. Edmond	Berthier
St. Edmond - Lac au Saumon	Matapedia
St. Edmond de Coaticook	Stanstead
St. Edmond de Stoneham	Quebec
St. Edouard de Frampton	Dorchester
St. Edouard de Gentilly	Nicolet
St. Edouard de Knowlton	Brome
St. Edouard	I'lle Montreal
St. Edouard	Lotbiniere
St. Edouard	Maskinonge
St. Edouard	Napierville
St. Edouard - Fabre	Temiscamingue
St. Edward - Knowlton	Brome
St. Eleuthere	Kamouraska
St. Elie de Caxton	St. Maurice
St. Elie d'Orford	Sherbrooke
St. Eloi	Riviere du Loup
St. Elphegie	Yamaska
St. Elzear de Liniere	Beauce
St. Elezar - I'lle Jesus	Laval
St. Emile	Montcalm
St. Emile - Suffolk	Papineau
St. Enfant Jesus du Mile End	I'lle Montreal
St. Ephrem de Tring	Beauce
St. Ephrem d'Upton	Bagot
St. Ephrem - Fitch Bay	Stanstead
St. Epiphane	Riviere du Loup
St. Esprit	Montcalm
St. Etienne	Beauharnois
St. Etienne de Beaumont	Bellechasse
St. Etienne de Bolton	Brome

St. Etienne de Chelsea	Gatineau
St. Etienne de la Malbaie	Charlevoix Est
St. Etienne de Lauzon	Levis
St. Etienne de Gres	St. Maurice
St. Eugene - Grantham	Drummond
St. Eugene	L'Islet
St. Eugene - Guigues	Temiscamingue
St. Eupheme	Montmagny
St. Eusebe - Stanfold	Arthabaska
St. Eusebe - Vercil	I'lle Montreal
St. Eustache	Deux Montagnes
St. Evariste de Forsyth	Beauce
St. Fabien de Panet	Montmagny
St. Fabien	Rimouski
St. Faustin	Terrebonne
St. Felicien	Lac St. Jean Quest
St. Felix de Cap Rouge	Quebec
St. Felix de Valois	Joliette
St. Felix de Valois - Cheneville	Papineau
St. Felix de Valois - Kingsey	Drummond
St. Ferdinand d'Halifax - Bernierville	Megantic
St. Ferreol les Neiges	Montmorency #1
St. Fidele de Mount Murray	Charlevoix Est
St. Flavien	Lotbiniere
St. Fortunat - Wolfestown	Wolfe
St. Francois d'Assise	Beauce
St. Francois d'Assise - Frelighsburg	Missisquoi
St. Francois d'Assise-Longue Pte.	I'lle Montreal
St. Francois d'Assise	Ottawa
St. Francois de la Riviere Sud	Montmagny
St. Francois de Sales - I.O.	Montmorency #2
St. Francois de Sales-I'lle Jesus	Laval
St. Francois de Sales-Neuville	Portneuf
St. Francois de Sales-Pt.Gatineau	Hull
St. Francois de Sales	Lac St. Jean Ouest
St. Francois du Lac	Yamaska
St. Francis Xavier	Pontiac
St. Francois Xavier	Yamaska
St. Francois Xavier - Bassin	Iles de la Madeleine
St. Francois Xavier-Batiscan	Champlain
St. Francois Xavier	Chicoutimi
St. Francois Xavier-Petite Riviere	Charlevoix Quest
St. Francois Xavier - Brompton	Richmond
St. Francois Xavier	Vercheres
St. Francois Xavier de Viger	Riviere du Loup
St. Francois Xavier-West Shefford	Shefford
St. Francois Xavier-Sault St. Louis	Laprairie
St. Frederic	Beauce
St. Frederic	Drummond
St. Fulgence de Durham	Drummond
St. Fulgence-l'Anse aux Foins	Chicoutimi
St. Gabriel	Rimouski
St. Gabriel - Bouchette	Gatineau
St. Gabriel - Brandon	Berthier
St. Gabriel - Stratford	Wolfe

St. Gabriel - Valcartier	Quebec
St. Gabriel - Guerin	Temiscamingue
St. Gabriel's Parish	Montreal
St. Gedeon	Beauce
St. Gedeon	Lac St. Jean Est
St. Georges d'Aubert Gallion	Beauce
St. Georges	Champlain
St. Georges - Mingan	Saguenay
St. Georges de Cacouna	Riviere du Loup
St. Georges de Malbaie	Gaspe East
St. Georges de Noyan	Iberville
St. Georges de Port Daniel	Bonaventure
St. Georges de Windsor	Richmond
St. Germain de Grantham	Drummond
St. Germain	Kamouraska
St. Germain	Rimouski
St. Gilbert - Deschambault	Portneuf
St. Gilles de Beaurivage	Lotbiniere
St. Godefroi	Bonaventure
St. Gregoire de Montmorency	Montmorency #1
St. Gregoire de Nazianze	Papineau
St. Gregoire le Grand	Iberville
St. Gregoire le Grand	Nicolet
St. Guillaume d'Upton	Drummond
St. Henri - East Hereford	Compton
St. Henri de Lauzon	Levis
St. Henri de Mascouche	L'Assomption
St. Henri des Tanneries	I'lle Montreal
St. Hermas	Deux Montagnes
St. Hermenegilde	Stanstead
St. Hilaire	Rouville
St. Hilarion	Charlevoix Quest
St. Hippolyte - Riviere au Tonnerre	Saguenay
St. Hippolyte de Kilkenny	Terrebonne
St. Hippolyte de Wotton	Wolfe
St. Honore	Chicoutimi
St. Honore	Temiscouata
St. Honore de Shenley	Beauce
St. Hubert	Chambly
St. Hubert	Riviere du Loup
St. Hugues	Bagot
St. Hyacinthe	St. Hyacinthe
St. Hyacinthe le Confesseur	St. Hyacinthe
St. Ignance - Stanbridge	Missisquoi
St. Ignance de Coteau du Lac	Soulanges
St. Ignance de Loyola	Berthier
St. Ignance du Cap St. Ignance	Montmagny
St. Ignance du Lac	Maskinonge
St. Irenee	Charlevoix Est
St. Isidore	Laprairie
St. Isidore de Lauzon	Dorchester
St. Isidore - Laverlochere	Temiscamingue
St. Jacques (Cathedrale)	I'lle Montreal
St. Jacques - Causapscal	Matapedia
St. Jacques - Parisville	Lotbiniere

St. Jacques de l'Achigan	Montcalm
St. Jacques de Leeds	Megantic
St. Jacques le Majeur	Montreal
St. Jacques le Majeur - Clarenceville	Missisquoi
St. Jacques le Majeur	Abitibi
St. Jacques le Majeur	Pontiac
St. Jacques le Mineur	Laprarie
St. Jacques le Mineur - Dupuy	Abitibi
St. James - Port Daniel	Bonaventure
St. James the Great	Pontiac
St. Janvier-Blainville (Mirabel)	Terrebonne
St. Janvier-Weedon	Wolfe
St. Jean I.O.	Montmorency #2
St. Jean Baptiste - Hochlega	I'lle Montreal
St. Jean Baptiste	Lotbiniere
St. Jean Baptiste de l'Anse	Lac St. Jean Quest
St. Jean Baptiste I.O.	Montmorency #2
St. Jean Baptiste-I'lle Verte	Riviere du Loup
St. Jean Baptiste	Nicolet
St. Jean Baptiste	Quebec
St. Jean Baptiste	Rouville
St. Jean Baptiste	Sherbrooke
St. Jean Baptiste-Roxton Falls	Shefford
St. Jean Baptiste-Ecureuils	Portneuf
St. Jean Chrysostome	Chateauguay
St. Jean Chrysostome-Lauzon	Levis
St. Jean de Dieu	I'lle Montreal
St. Jean de Dieu	Riviere du Loup
St. Jean Deschaillons	Lotbiniere
St. Jean Francois Regis	Laprairie
St. Jean Francois Regis	Huntingdon
St. Jean l'Evangeliste (Cathedrale)	St. Jean
St. Jean l'Evangeliste - Nouvelle	Bonaventure
St. Jean l'Evangeliste - Thurso	Papineau
St. Jean l'Evangeliste - Wickham	Drummond
St. Jean l'Evangeliste - Macamic	Abitibi
St. Jean l'Evangeliste - Coaticook	Stanstead
St. Jean Matha	Joliette
St. Jean Port Joli	L'Islet
St. Jean sur Richelieu	St. Jean
St. Jerome	Lac St. Jean Est
St. Jerome (Cathedrale)	Terrebonne
St. Jerome	Matane
St. Jerome	Lac St. Jean
St. Joachim	Montmorency #1
St. Joachim	Chateauguay
St. Joachim - Pointe Claire	I'lle Montreal
St. Joachim	Ottawa
St. Joachim	Shefford
St. Joachim de Courval	Yamaska
St. John Evangeliste - Quyon	Pontiac
St. Joseph - Montreal	I'lle Montreal
St. Joseph	Beauce
St. Joseph - Wrightville	Hull
St. Joseph	Ottawa

St. Joseph	Richelieu
St. Joseph	St. Hyacinthe
St. Joseph d'Alma	Lac St. Jean Est
St. Joseph de Cap d'Espoir	Gaspe East
St. Joseph - Carleton	Bonaventure
St. Joseph	Chambly
St. Joseph - Deschambault	Portneuf
St. Joseph	Huntingdon
St. Joseph - Lanoraie	Berthier
St. Joseph - Tabatiere	Saguenay
St. Joseph - Notre Dame du Nord	Temiscamingue
St. Joseph de Ham Sud	Wolfe
St. Joseph de la Pointe Levy	Levis
St. Joseph de la Riviere des Praries	I'lle Montreal
St. Joseph de Lepage	Rimouski
St. Joseph d'Ely	Shefford
St. Joseph	Maskinonge
St. Joseph de Moisie	Saguenay
St. Joseph de Soulanges	Soulanges
St. Joseph de Wakefield	Gatineau
St. Joseph du Lac	Deux Montagnes
St. Jovite	Terrebonne
St. Jude	St. Hyacinthe
St. Jude - Authier	Abitibi
St. Julien - Wolfestown	Wolfe
St. Justin	Maskinonge
St. Lambert	Chambly
St. Lambert - Lauzon	Levis
St. Laurent	I'lle Montreal
St. Laurent I.O.	Montmorency #2
St. Lazare	Bellechasse
St. Lazare	Vaudreuil
St. Leon - Val Racine	Frontenac
St. Leon de Standon	Dorchester
St. Leon le Grand	Maskinonge
St. Leon le Grand	Matapedia
St. Leonard - Port Maurice	I'lle Montreal
St. Leonard d'Aston	Nicolet
St. Leonard	Portneuf
St. Liboire de Ramezay	Bagot
St. Ligouri	Montcalm
St. Lin des Laurentides	L'Assomption
St. Louis	Kamouraska
St. Louis	Lotbiniere
St. Louis	St. Maurice
St. Louis	Terrebonne
St. Louis - Isle aux Coudres	Charlevoix Quest
St. Louis de Blanford	Arthabaska
St. Louis de Bonsecours	Richelieu
St. Louis de France	Champlain
St. Louis de France - East Angus	Compton
St. Louis de France	I'lle Montreal
St. Louis de France	Terrebonne
St. Louis de France - N. D. du Nord	Temiscamingue
St. Louis de Gonzague	Beauharnois

St. Louis de Pintendre	Levis
St. Louis de Poltimore	Papineau
St. Louis de Ville Forges	St. Maurice
St. Louis de Metabetchouan	Lac St. Jean Est
St, Louis du Ha!Ha!	Temiscouata
St. Luc	Matane
St. Luc	St. Jean
St. Luc - La Motte	Abitibi
St. Luc - Disraeli	Wolfe
St. Luc de la Grosse Ile	Montmagny
St. Luc de Vincennes	Champlain
St. Lucien	Drummond
St. Ludger	Frontenac
St. Magliore de Roux	Bellechasse
St. Majorique - Grantham	Drummond
St. Malachie	Otawa
St. Malachie	Papineau
St. Malachie de Frampton	Dorchester
St. Malachie d'Ormstown	Chateauguay
St. Malo	Compton
St. Malo	Quebec
St. Marcellin Les Escoumins	Saguenay
St. Marcel de Richelieu	Richelieu
St. Marcel	L'Islet
St. Marc - Coaticook	Stanstead
St. Marc de Cournoyer	Vercheres
St. Marc sur Richelieu	Vercheres
St. Martin	Beauce
St. Martin - Martinville	Compton
St. Martin de I'lle Jesus	Laval
St. Martin de Riviere au Renard	Gaspe East
St. Mathias	Rouville
St. Mathieu	Laprarie
St. Mathieu de Beloeil	Vercheres
St. Mathieu de Dixville	Stanstead
St. Mathieu - Lac Bellemare	St. Maurice
St, Mathieu de Rioux	Rimouski
St. Maurice	Champlain
St. Maxime - Scott	Dorchester
St. Maxime du Mont Louis	Gaspe West
St. Medard - Coteau Station	Soulanges
St. Medard de Warwick	Arthabaska
St. Methode	Frontenac
St. Methode	Lac St. Jean Ouest
St, Michel - Rougemont	Rouville
St. Michel (Cathedrale)	Sherbrooke
St. Michel (St. Colomb)	Quebec
St. Michel Archange	Quebec
St. Michel Archange	Napierville
St. Michel Archange - Rouyn	Temiscamingue
St. Michel de la Durantaye	Bellechasse
St. Michel de Perce	Gaspe East
St. Michel des Forges	St. Maurice
St. Michel des Saints	Berthier
St. Michel de Wentworth	Argenteuil

St, Michel	Vaudreuil
St. Michel	Yamaska
St. Michel's Chapel - Sillery	Quebec
St. Modeste	Riviere du Loup
St. Moise	Matapedia
St. Narcisse	Champlain
St. Narcisse de Beaurivage	Lotbiniere
St. Nazaire d'Acton	Bagot
St, Neree	Bellechasse
St. Nicholas	Levis
St. Nom de Marie - Sayabec	Matapedia
St. Nom de Marie - Marieville	Rouville
St. Nom de Marie - Lac St. Marie	Gatineau
St. Norbert	Berthier
St. Norbert	Arthabaska
St. Norbert - Cap Chat	Gaspe West
St. Octave - Dosquet	Lotbiniere
St. Octave de Magpie	Saguenay
St. Octave de Metis	Matane
St. Odilion de Cranbourne	Dorchester
St. Omer	Bonaventure
St. Onesime	Kamouraska
St. Ours	Richelieu
St. Pacome	Kamouraska
St. Pamphile	L'Islet
St. Pascal	Kamouraska
St. Patrice de Beaurivage	Lotbiniere
St. Patrice - Hinchinbrooke	Huntingdon
St. Patrice	Riviere du Loup
St. Patrice de Magog	Stanstead
St. Patrice de Rawdon	Montcalm
St. Patrice de Sherrington	Napierville
St. Patrice de Tingwick	Arthabaska
St. Patrice - Montreal	I'lle Montreal
St. Patrick - Quebec City	Quebec
St. Patrick	Sherbrooke
St. Patrick's - Douglastown	Gaspe East
St. Paul - Scotstown	Compton
St. Paul - Senneterre	Abitibi
St. Paul d'Abbotsford	Rouville
St. Paul d'Aylmer	Gatineau
St. Paul de Chester	Arthabaska
St. Paul de Grand Mere	Champlain
St. Paul de la Croix	Riviere du Loup
St. Paul de Lavaltrie	Joliette
St. Paul de Montminy	Montmagny
St. Paul I'le Aux Noix	St. Jean
St. Paul - Montreal	I'lle Montreal
St. Paul du Nord	Saguenay
St. Paul l'Ermite	L'Assomption
St. Paul the Ermit - Sheenboro	Pontiac
St. Paul's - Shawville	Pontiac
St. Paulin	Maskinonge
St. Philemon	Bellechasse
St. Philemon de Stoke	Richmond

139

St. Philippe	Laprairie
St. Philippe	Argenteuil
St. Philippe - Philipsburg	Missisquoi
St. Philippe - La Reine	Abitibi
St. Philippe de Neri	Kamouraska
St. Philippe de Windsor	Richmond
St. Pie	Bagot
St. Pie de Guire	Yamaska
St. Pierre - Etang du Nord	Iles de la Madeleine
St. Pierre	Saguenay
St. Pierre - Taschereau	Abitibi
St. Pierre - Fort Coulonge	Pontiac
St. Pierre aux Leins	I'lle Montreal
St. Pierre de Baptiste	Megantic
St. Pierre de Broughton	Beauce
St. Pierre de Durham	Drummond
St. Pierre de la Patrie	Compton
St. Pierre de la Pte. aux Esquimaux	Saguenay
St. Pierre de la Riviere Sud	Montmagny
St. Pierre I.O.	Montmorency #2
St. Pierre de Malbaie	Gaspe East
St. Pierre de Shawinigan	St. Maurice
St. Pierre de Sorel	Richelieu
St. Pierre de Portage	L'Assomption
St. Pierre de Wakefield	Gatineau
St. Pierre de Verrone - Pike River	Missisquoi
St. Pierre du Lac - Val Brillant	Matapedia
St. Pierre et St. Paul - Baie St. Paul	Charlevoix Quest
St. Pierre les Becquets	Nicolet
St. Placide	Charlevoix Quest
St. Placide	Deux Montagnes
St. Placide - Bern	Temiscamingue
St. Polycarpe	Soulanges
St. Prime	Lac St. Jean Quest
St. Prosper	Champlain
St. Prosper	Dorchester
St. Raphael	Bellechasse
St. Raphael - Albertville	Matapedia
St. Raphael de Bury	Compton
St. Raphael de I'lle Bizard	I'lle Montreal
St. Raymond - Nonnat	Portneuf
St. Regis	Huntingdon
St. Remi de la Salle	Napierville
St. Remi de Tingwick	Arthabaska
St. Remi - Lac au Sable	Portneuf
St. Robert	Richelieu
St. Roc - Rock Forest	Sherbrooke
St. Roch de l'Achigan	L'Assomption
St. Roch des Aulnaies	L'Islet
St. Roch	Quebec
St. Roch	Richelieu
St. Romain de Winslow	Frontenac
St. Romain de Hemmingford	Huntingdon
St. Romuald de Farnham	Missisquoi
St. Romuald d'Etchemin	Levis

St. Rosairie	Arthabaska
St. Samuel	Frontenac
St. Samuel	Nicolet
St. Sauveur	Quebec
St. Sauveur des Monts	Terrebonne
St. Sebastien	Beauce
St. Sebastien	Iberville
St. Severe	St. Maurice
St. Severe - Proulxville	Champlain
St. Severin	Beauce
St. Simeon	Charlevoix Est
St. Simon	Bagot
St. Simon	Rimouski
St. Simon - Vilemontel	Abitibi
St, Sixte	Papineau
St. Stanislas - Ascot	Sherbrooke
St. Stanislas de Kostka	Beauharnois
St. Stanislas - Riviere des Envies	Champlain
St. Stephen - Old Chelsea	Gatineau
St. Sulpice	L'Assomption
St. Sylvere	Nicolet
St. Sylvestre	Lotbiniere
St. Telesphore	Soulanges
St. Thecle	Champlain
St. Theodore d'Acton	Bagot
St. Theodore - Grand 'Anse	Champlain
St. Theodore de Chertsey	Montcalm
St. Theophile	Beauce
St. Theophile d'Ely - Racine	Shefford
St. Theophile du Lac - Lac a la Tortue	Champlain
St. Thomas	Joliette
St. Thomas d'Aquin	Compton
St. Thomas d'Aquin	Lac St. Jean Quest
St. Thomas d'Aquin	St. Hyacinthe
St. Thomas d'Aquin - Hudson	Vaudreuil
St. Thomas - Pointe a la Caille	Montmagny
St. Thomas de Caxton	St. Maurice
St. Thomas de Pierreville	Yamaska
St. Thuribe	Portneuf
St. Timothee	Beauharnois
St. Timothee d'Herouxville	Champlain
St. Tite	Champlain
St. Tite des Caps	Montmorency #1
St. Ubald	Portneuf
St. Ulric - Riviere Blanche	Matane
St. Urbain	Charlevoix Quest
St. Urbain	Chateauguay
St. Valentin	St. Jean
St. Valere	Arthabaska
St. Valerien	Rimouski
St. Valerien	Shefford
St. Vallier	Bellechasse
St. Venant d'Hereford	Compton
St. Victor de Tring	Beauce
St, Vincent de Paul - Montreal	I'lle Montreal

141

St. Vincent de Paul - I'lle Jesus	Laval
St. Vincent Ferrier - Adamsville	Brome
St. Vital	Saguenay
St. Vital - Lambton	Beauce
St. Wenceslas	Nicolet
St. Wilfred	Stanstead
St. Zacharie	Beauce
St. Zenon	Berthier
St. Zenon - Piopolis	Frontenac
St. Zenon - Lac Humqui	Matapedia
St. Zephirin de Courval	Yamaska
St. Zephirin de Stadacona	Quebec
St. Zotique	Soulanges
Ste. Adelaide de Pabos	Gaspe East
Ste. Adele	Terrebonne
Ste. Agathe	Lotbiniere
Ste. Agathe des Monts	Terrebonne
Ste. Agnes	Charlevoix Est
Ste. Agnes - Lac Megantic	Frontenac
Ste. Agnes de Dundee	Huntingdon
Ste. Anastasie - Lachute	Argenteuil
Ste. Anastasie de Nelson - Lyster	Megantic
Ste. Angele de Laval	Nicolet
Ste. Angele de Merici	Rimouski
Ste. Angele de Merici	Rouville
Ste. Angele de Monnoir	Rouville
Ste. Angele de Premont	Maskinonge
Ste. Angelique - Papineauville	Papineau
Ste. Anne - Sabrevois	Iberville
Ste. Ann - Montreal	I'lle Montreal
Ste. Anne	Ottawa
Ste. Anne de Beaupre	Montmorency #1
Ste. Anne de Bellevue	I'lle Montreal
Ste. Anne de Danville	Richmond
Ste. Anne de la Perade	Champlain
Ste. Anne de la Pocatiere	Kamouraska
Ste. Anne de la Rochelle	Shefford
Ste. Anne de Ristigouche	Bonaventure
Ste. Anne de Pointe au Peres	Rimouski
Ste. Anne de Sault	Arthabaska
Ste. Anne des Monts	Gaspe West
Ste. Anne de Sorel	Richelieu
Ste. Anne des Plaines	Terrebonne
Ste. Anne de Stukely	Shefford
Ste. Anne de Varennes	Vercheres
Ste. Anne du Bout de I'lle	I'lle Montreal
Ste. Anne du Grand Calumet	Pontiac
Ste. Anne du Saguenay	Chicoutimi
Ste. Anne d'Yamachiche	St. Maurice
Ste. Appoline	Montmagny
Ste. Barbe	Huntingdon
Ste. Beatrix	Joliette
Ste. Bernadette - Boileau	Chicoutimi
Ste. Bibiane de Cleveland	Richmond
Ste. Blandine	Rimouski

Ste. Brigide,- Montreal	I'lle Montreal
Ste. Brigide	Iberville
Ste. Brigide	Ottawa
Ste. Brigid's of North Onslow	Pontiac
Ste. Brigitte de Laval	Montmorency 1
Ste. Brigitte de Maria	Bonaventure
Ste. Brigitte des Saults	Nicolet
Ste. Catherine - Katevale	Stanstead
Ste. Catherine de Fossambault	Portneuf
Ste. Catherine de la Jacques Cartier	I'lle Montreal
Ste. Cecile de Cloridorme	Gaspe East
Ste. Cecile de Masham	Gatineau
Ste. Cecile de Milton	Shefford
Ste. Cecile de Valleyfield	Beauharnois
Ste. Cecile de Whitton	Frontenac
Ste. Cecile du Bic	Rimouski
Ste. Christine	Bagot
Ste. Christine	Portneuf
Ste. Claire	Dorchester
Ste. Claire de Assise - R. Beaudette	Soulanges
Ste. Claire de I'lle Percee	Gaspe East
Ste. Clothilde	Chateauguay
Ste. Clothilde de Horton	Arthabaska
Ste. Croix	Lotbiniere
Ste. Croix de Dunham	Missisquoi
Ste. Croix de Tadoussac	Saguenay
Ste. Cunegonde - Montreal	I'lle Montreal
Ste. Dorothee - I'lle Jesus	Laval
Ste. Edwidge	Compton
Ste. Elizabeth - Cantley	Gatineau
Ste. Elizabeth - Dautray	Joliette
Ste. Elizabeth - Vinton	Pontiac
Ste. Elizabeth - North Hatley	Stanstead
Ste. Elizabeth de Warwick	Arthabaska
Ste. Elizabeth de Portugal	I'lle Montreal
Ste. Emelie de l'Energie	Joliette
Ste. Emmelie	Lotbiniere
Ste. Eulalie	Nicolet
Ste. Famille d'Aumond	Gatineau
Ste. Famille de Boucherville	Chambly
Ste. Famille I.O.	Montmorency #2
Ste. Famille de Pabos	Gaspe East
Ste. Famille du Cap Sante	Portneuf
Ste. Felicite	Matane
Ste. Flavie	Rimouski
Ste. Flore - Grand Mere	Champlain
Ste. Florence	Matapedia
Ste. Foy	Quebec
Ste. Francoise	Temiscouata
Ste. Genevieve - Pierrefonds	I'lle Montreal
Ste. Genevieve - Batiscan	Champlain
Ste. Genevieve	Berthier
Ste. Germaine du Lac Etchemin	Dorchester
Ste. Gertrude	Nicolet
Ste. Hedwidge	Lac St. Jean Quest

Ste. Helene	Bagot
Ste. Helene de Chester	Arthabaska
Ste. Helene	Kamouraska
Ste. Henedine	Dorchester
Ste. Jeanne de Chantal - I'lle Perrot	Vaudreuil
Ste. Jeanne de Neuville	Portneuf
Ste. Julie	Vercheres
Ste. Julie de Somerset	Megantic
Ste. Julienne	Montcalm
Ste. Justine de Langevin	Dorchester
Ste. Justine de Newton	Vaudreuil
Ste. Louise des Aulnaies	L'Islet
Ste. Luce	Rimouski
Ste. Lucie	Terrebonne
Ste. Madeleine	St. Hyacinthe
Ste. Madeleine - Havre aux Maisons	Iles de la Madeleine
Ste. Madeleine - Rigaud	Vaudreuil
Ste. Madeleine de Riviere Madeleine	Gaspe West
Ste. Marguerite de Blairfindie	St. Jean
Ste. Marguerite de Jolliet	Dorchester
Ste. Marguerite - Lac Masson	Terrebonne
Ste. Marguerite Marie - Magog	Stanstead
Ste. Marie	Beauce
Ste. Marie de Blandford	Nicolet
Ste. Marie d'Ely - Maricourt	Shefford
Ste. Marie Grignon - I'le Jesus	Laval
Ste. Marie Madeleine	Gaspe West
Ste. Marie Madeleine	St. Hyacinthe
Ste. Marie Madeleine - Cap Madeleine	Champlain
Ste. Marie Mediatrice d'Estcourt	Temiscouata
Ste. Marie Solomee	Montcalm
Ste. Marthe	Vaudreuil
Ste. Martine	Chateauguay
Ste. Mary Quyon - North Onslow	Pontiac
Ste. Melanie d'Ailleboust	Joliette
Ste. Monique	Nicolet
Ste. Monique	Deux Montagnes
Ste. Perpetue	L'Islet
Ste. Perpetue	Nicolet
Ste. Petronille de Beaulieu I.O.	Montmorency #2
Ste. Philomene - Ville Mercier	Chateauguay
Ste. Philomene - Fortierville	Lotbiniere
Ste. Praxede de Brompton Falls	Richmond
Ste. Prudentinne de Roxton Pond	Shefford
Ste. Rosalie	Bagot
Ste. Rose de Degele	Temiscouata
Ste. Rose de I'lle Jesus	Laval
Ste. Rose de Lima	Papineau/Hull
Ste. Rose de Lima - Cowansville	Missisquoi
Ste. Rose de Lima - Sweetsburg	Missisquoi
Ste. Rose de Watford	Dorchester
Ste. Rose du Nord	Chicoutimi
Ste. Sabine	Missisquoi
Ste. Scholastique - Mirabel	Deux Montagnes
Ste. Sophie	Terrebonne

Ste. Sophie - East Aldfield	Pontiac
Ste. Sophie de Levrard	Nicolet
Ste. Sophie de Halifax - Halifax Nord	Megantic
Ste. Suzanne de Stanhope	Stanstead
Ste. Theodosie - Calixa Lavalee	Vercheres
Ste. Therese d'Avila	Terrebonne
Ste. Therese - Beebe Plain	Stanstead
Ste. Therese - Cowansville	Missisquoi
Ste. Therese de Blainville	Terrebonne
Ste. Therese - Amos	Abitibi
Ste. Trinite	Vercheres
Ste. Ursule	Maskinonge
Ste. Valerie - Boileau	Papineau
Ste. Veronique	LaBelle
Ste. Victorie	Richelieu
Ste. Victorie - Sorel	Richelieu
Ste. Victorie - Victoriaville	Arthabaska
Sts. Anges	Beauce
Sts. Anges de Lachine	I'lle Montreal
Sts. Anges Gardiens de Cascapediac	Bonaventure
Sts. Gervais et Protais	Bellechasse
Sts. Sept Freres - Grosses Roches	Matane
Soeurs du Bon Pasteur - Pont Viau	I'lle Jesus
Tadoussac - Postes du Domaine du Roi	Saguenay
Taschereau	Abitibi
Tadoussac - Ste. Croix	Saguenay
Terrebonne	Terrebonne
Thurso	Papineau
Tingwick	Arthabaska
Tracadieche	Bonaventure
Tres St. Nom de Jesus	I'lle Montreal
Tres Ste Trinite - Contrecoeur	Vercheres
Tres St. Redempteur	Hull
Tres St. Redempteur	Vaudreuil
Tres St. Sacrement - Howick	Chateauguay
Tres Sts. Anges de Ham Nord	Wolfe
Trinity	Iberville
Trois Pistoles	Riviere du Loup
Trois Rivieres	St. Maurice
Upton	Bagot
Val Brillant	Matapedia
Valcourt	Shefford
Val des Bois	Papineau
Val des Monts	Hull
Val Jalbert	Lac St. Jean Ouest
Valmont	Champlain
Varennes	Vercheres
Vaudreuil	Vaudreuil
Vercheres	Vercheres
Verdun	I'lle Montreal
Victoriaville	Arthabaska
Vilemontel	Abitibi
Villeneuve	Quebec
Warwick	Arthabaska
Waterloo	Shefford

Weedon Centre	Wolfe
Wickham	Drummond
Windsor	Richmond
Wolf Lake	Pontiac
Wottonville	Wolfe
Yamachiche	St. Maurice
Yamaska	Yamaska